T0333861

THE MOST
INTERESTING
BOOK
IN THE WORLD*

*Weird, isn't it, how the half-title page is always blank except for the title of the book, which you've just seen on the cover and which will be presented in full on *literally the next page*. So why is it here? The half-title used to be known as the 'bastard title', shielding its legitimate brother, the title page, from dirt on the text block's journey from the printer to bookbinder. The bastard also served another practical use. Until about 300 years ago, the custom was to store books on shelves fore-edges out, with their spines to the wall. Their titles were then written in ink on their fore-edges, not the spines – or you tore the bastard title out of the book and pasted it onto the fore-edge of the book to identify it. Then came what historians call the 'Great Turnaround', when the fashion changed – bibliophiles wanted to see their fine gilt-stamped spines, and books were shelved in reverse, as they are today. Even though the bastard title is redundant, modern books like this one still carry it, like a vestigial tail. Anyway, on to the next page. I WONDER WHAT IT COULD BE …

THE MOST
INTERES
BOOK
IN THE
WO

To my parents,
whose love of interesting things created a curious thing.

TING

A miscellany of things too strange to be true, yet somehow are

RLD

by Edward Brooke-Hitching

**SIMON &
SCHUSTER**

London · New York · Sydney · Toronto · New Delhi

MMXXIV

INTRODUCTION

'When you run into something interesting, drop

Look, I know what you're thinking. In all likelihood it's something along the lines of *What kind of pompous idiot declares his book to be the* most *interesting?*[1] The thing is, I knew the idea would be trouble the moment I jotted it down years ago. Which is why I immediately started writing it.

This is a book for everyone, everywhere, interested in anything. It's a book that started life as a box. Labelled 'Interesting Things', it was begun as a hobby while growing up in a rare bookshop as the son of an antiquarian dealer. From maps showing South American giants, to witch-hunting manuals, to shipwreck diaries written in penguin blood, every kind of oddity crosses the rare-book counter at one time or another. Like a caffeinated lepidopterist[2] you feel compelled to net and note down every variety of the curious and peculiar, with no particular agenda

1. Firstly, the word 'idiot' comes from the Greek noun *idiōtēs* meaning 'private citizen', which means it's perfectly accurate to describe me and indeed the vast majority of ancient Greeks as complete idiots, should you wish to do so. (Secondly, how *dare* you.)

2. Incidentally, an unexpected significant figure in the history of the study of butterflies and moths is the author Vladimir Nabokov, whose obsession with butterfly genitals led him (with eleven novels already to his name) to volunteer at Harvard University's Museum of Comparative Zoology, spending fourteen-hour shifts producing thousands of illustrations of butterfly sexual organs and naming new species. He even formed a theory about the Chilean genus *Polyommatus*, that it had originated in Asia and reached the New World via Siberia and the Bering Strait. Contemporary experts scoffed at the idea; yet in 2011 DNA evidence proved him right.

·verything else and study it.' B. F. Skinner (1904-1990)

other than to simply record their existence before they disappear again behind the closed doors of private collections.

When I moved to London to work for an auctioneering company, Interesting Things and its bulk of notebooks, folders and hard drives came with me, and it was a note from these that gave me the idea for my first book, *Fox Tossing, Octopus Wrestling and Other Forgotten Sports*. Subsequent books have been both inspired and fattened by its ever-growing scraps of notes, photocopies, newspaper clippings, academic articles and illustrations along the way. This caught the attention of the producers of the BBC TV show *QI*, for whom I researched and wrote scripts for six series of the show as a so-called 'QI Elf'.[3]

But it's with this book that the Interesting Things have their own volume, spilling out across the pages of a compilation devoted solely to the most fascinating information. This is, of course, a tricky metric to apply because, like attractiveness, interestingness is thought of as subjective. (If beauty is in the eye of the beholder, then interest is in the eye of the book-holder.) But this compendium is built on the idea that this is only true up to a point, because some things – like the petrichor scent of woodland after rainfall, or the swelling harmony of an orchestra warming up – are just objectively, undeniably beautiful. And some things are indisputably interesting: whether it's the fact that sharks are older than trees (see page 134); or that Siberian trees turn to glass to survive the winter (see page 297). That in 2017 the geographical centre of North America was

3. An odd job title to be sure, but infinitely preferable to the official term for someone who collects such material, the hazardously misleading 'spermatologist' (collector of seeds).

discovered to be – by complete coincidence – the town of Center, North Dakota (see page 219). That inside edible figs is a dead wasp (see page 227), or that a dead King Tutankhamun was mummified with a ninety-degree erection *and* appears to have spontaneously combusted inside his sarcophagus (see page 49). Things like these prod the brain's curiosity cortex like pokers stirring embers, and the hope is that with this book you will be provided with the greatest possible density of interestingness-per-square-inch that a book can wrestle between its boards. 'Curiosity is the thirst of the soul; it inflames and torments us, and makes us taste every thing with joy,' wrote Samuel Johnson (who no doubt would have added that this goes double for flaming pharaohs with raging stiffies had he thought of it at the time).[4]

In keeping with the poor decision-making responsible for the outrageous title of this book, and indeed the previous sentence, this is a volume of calculated risks. There are no chapters, for one. Honestly, it felt like they would just get in the way. Rather than corral the fidgeting material into fifteen or so vague categories, risking both repetition and a more pleasant reading experience, instead a kind of magnetised chaos was plumped for, in the true spirit of the miscellany genre (and what the poet Louis MacNeice called 'the drunkenness of things being various').

Each curious story, fact, or illustration is slotted beside a thematically connected companion in a great chain that leads around the world and back and forth through time. This loosely threaded mayhem is

---

4. According to James Boswell, Samuel Johnson would boast that his memory was so capacious that he could recite an entire chapter of Niels Horrebow's *The Natural History of Iceland* (1758). This chapter is, in full: 'Chap. LXXII. Concerning Snakes. There are no snakes to be met with throughout the whole island.' (Chapter XLII is even shorter, commenting similarly on the lack of owls.)

The curiosity room of Italian apothecary Ferrante Imperato, a collection of his own 'interesting things', at the Palazzo Gravina in Naples in 1599.

what I have always loved about the genre. A miscellany should be a paper wonder-palace to be explored endlessly, with hallways so long and winding and madly decorated that you happily resign yourself to its labyrinth. Repeat readings should be rewarded, so that on each browsing one finds new things to savour. You'll notice this philosophy in several excessive features – the overabundance of footnotes, for one. Sometimes there are footnotes to these footnotes ('toe-notes', can we call them?), like scribbled napkins spilling from an obsessive's pocket.[5]

---

5. The English Literature professor Thomas McFarland tried to have his publisher release his book without a single footnote, because to him they made reading feel 'like driving over a road with unnumerable potholes', and were only there 'to allow scholarly readers to purloin my citations without having to give me a reference'.*

  McFarland would have been horrified by the Foot notes of nineteenth-century poet Edward Edwin Foot, who felt the need to explain every single phrase and metaphor he used. His footnotes to the first two lines of his elegy to Lord Palmerston were longer than the entire poem itself.

  *So long as we're footnoting footnotes it should be mentioned that the record for doing this is held by the Victorian orientalist Henry Yule, whose translation of Marco Polo's *Travels* famously (in footnoting circles) features a footnote to a footnote to a footnote.*

  *Breaking Yule's record by inserting this quadruple footnote was simply too tempting an opportunity to pass up.

Whether it's the story of the hair-cutting bandit known as the Phantom Barber of Pascagoula (see page 126); the pirates who rode sheep (see page 94); how Kurt Vonnegut's father lifted a seven-storey building into the air, or his brother's involvement with a chicken cannon (see page 218); or the story of how Jesus Christ secretly fled from crucifixion to live a long life in Japan (where today you can find his grave and accompanying gift shop, see pages 85-86), over time each Interesting Thing snapped into place beside its thematic neighbour like Lego bricks in a washing machine.[6]

My sincere hope is that this book will provide entertainment and distraction with plenty to find interesting on just about everything; and ultimately come as close as possible to fulfilling the promise of its title.

KEY TO SYMBOLS USED IN THIS BOOK

💡 Inventions and theories   🧪 Science and medicine

🧍 The body   🌍 Geography   🪐 Space   🖋 Letters, books and documents   🎭 Entertainment   🐾 Animals and creatures

♀♂ Love and sex   ☠ Death and the after-life   ⚔ War

🏛 Politics, money and power   🍽 Food and drink

☦ Religion   🚉 Transport   🍁 Plants   🖌 Arts

---

6. A curious paper published in 2013 by the Department of Mathematics and Computer Science of Germany's Friedrich-Schiller University is *Random Structures from Lego Bricks*, in which a group of doctoral students describe stuffing a washing machine full of Lego bricks and repeatedly setting it on seventy-minute cycles at forty degrees Celsius to observe what, if any, random complex structures were formed by the end of the 'brick washing'. 'Future will show if this report is the starting point of a lively development, or some isolated strange event,' concluded the paper's slightly mad-sounding author Dr Ingo Althöfer.

SOME INTERESTING NUMBERS BEFORE WE GET STARTED

0
Population of the town of Nothing, Arizona, USA.

0.5
Per cent of the global male population descended from Genghis Khan.

0.7
Per cent of the global population that are drunk *right now*.

2
Number of chromosomes a potato has more than a human.

2
Per cent of Belgians who know their national anthem.

2
Number of psychiatrists working in Liberia at the time of writing.

2
Number of hats often worn concurrently by Leo Tolstoy.

3
Number of kneecaps possessed by the tennis player Andy Murray.

4
Number of nipples possessed by the singer Harry Styles.

6

Total number of years that the average person spends dreaming.

007

Dialling code used by someone in Britain to call someone in Russia.

10

Per cent of surveyed Americans that believe HTML is a sexually transmitted disease.

19

Number of swords the nineteenth-century showman Chevalier Cliquot could swallow simultaneously.

20

Number of the largest ships in the world that together produce more pollution than all the world's cars combined.

20

Per cent of British teenagers who think Winston Churchill is a fictional character.

28

Litres of blood drawn from Saddam Hussein to use as ink to write his own Qur'an.

30

Duration in minutes of a male ladybird's orgasm.

30

Average number of tornadoes reported in the UK each year.

42.5

Per cent of *The Last Supper* that is Leonardo's remaining original work.

43

Number of injured participants at the 2020 Mexican 'Festival of the Exploding Hammers', where people hit things with explosive-strapped hammers.

50

Per cent of human DNA shared with bananas.

54

Number of chromosomes a carp has more than a human.

55

Number of Maltesers that Ed Sheeran can fit into his mouth.

67

Number of microbe species living in the average belly button[7].

---

7. One 2012 study conducted in North Carolina, USA, of sixty belly buttons found a total of 2368 different species. Some 1458 of them were new to science. One subject had a rare bacterium in their belly button that was thought to exist only in Japanese soil, despite the fact they had never been to Japan. Two others had bacteria that are usually found on icecaps and in thermal vents. Not a single bacterium was common to all buttons.*

  *What to do with this information? Well, if you were the London biolab Open Cell, in 2019 you'd collect bacteria from celebrity belly buttons, armpits, ears and noses, with the aim of making cheese. Cheddar was made from Suggs, singer of the ska band Madness. Cheshire cheese was grown from Alex James, bassist for the band Blur. Rapper Professor Green, who stated a hatred of cheese, had his belly-button bacteria turned into mozzarella, which was the only cheese he considered bearable. The human dairy products were exhibited at London's Victoria and Albert Museum.

75

Per cent of silent-era movies that are lost
(50 per cent of sound-era films made pre-1950 are lost).

86

Per cent of Fortune 500 executives that cheat at golf.

92

Per cent of the Chinese population who are lactose intolerant.

97.5

Per cent of DNA shared by humans and mice.

106

Number of acres spanned by a single tree named Pando,
a male quaking aspen, in Utah, USA.

145

Number of soiled underpants that Tutankhamun was buried with.

320

Amount of times more powerful that the bite of a Galapagos ground
finch, pound-for-pound, is than the bite of a *Tyrannosaurus rex*.

375

Number of days the average person spends doing
laundry in their lifetime.

404

Largest number of people to have dressed as Albert Einstein
in one gathering.

400

Number of years the Chinese were printing with moveable type before Gutenberg.

421

Number of Scottish words for snow.

616

The number of the Beast given in the earliest copy of the Book of Revelation, not 666 as commonly thought.

1152.16

Length in metres of the longest salami ever made, by the Belgian company Cock's Meats.

1511

The heart rate in beats per minute (about twenty-five times per second) of the Etruscan shrew.

3417

Diameter of Hell in miles as estimated by Galileo Galilei in 1588.

10,000

Number of homing pigeons that underwent 'anal security check for suspicious objects' ahead of China's National Day celebrations in 2014.

100,000

Average number of boomerangs imported from Great Britain by Australia annually.

400,000

Average annual number of Shanghai citizens who engage
in pet cricket fights.

1,200,000

Average number of people in the air at any given time.

2,000,000

The average age in years of the soil in your garden.

2,400,000

Number of children's lives saved by Australian James Harrison,
who donated his rare type of blood plasma every three weeks
between 1954 and 2018.

2,500,000

Number of Mills & Boon novels mixed into the foundation
of the UK's M6 toll road to help bind the asphalt.

129,864,880

Number of existing book titles as estimated by the
Google Books initiative.

225,000,000

Number of years it would take to walk a light year.

5 billion

Number of skin cells a human sheds in twenty-four hours –
our skin regenerates every twenty-eight days.

SOME INTERESTING EVENTS BEFORE WE GET STARTED

15 January 1965 George and Charlotte Blonsky of New York successfully file a patent for their invention of a bed that spins a mother in labour around at such high speed that the infant is propelled out of the birth canal by centrifugal force and is caught by an 'infant reception net'.

20 January 1993 A suspicious-looking package is found outside a Territorial Army (TA) centre in Bristol, UK. The TA call the police, who call an army bomb disposal unit, which blows the box up. The content is discovered to be leaflets on how to deal with suspicious-looking packages.

15 February This is the annually celebrated 'John Frum Day' on the remote South Pacific island of Tanna. Devotees in the village of Lamakara believe that a mythical American named John Frum will one day arrive and provide them with houses, clothes, watches, cars and Coca-Cola.

22 February 1983 The first and only performance of *Moose Murders*, a 'mystery farce' that's so bad that it closes on its opening night and is widely regarded as the worst play ever staged. Its author, Arthur Bicknell, is spotted in the street by a member of the audience, who shouts 'Officer, arrest that show!'[8]

---

8. A close second is the debut performance on 10 December 1806 of *Mr H.*, a play by Charles Lamb, which was booed not only by the audience but also its author. The critic Crabb Robinson noted that Lamb 'was probably the loudest hisser in the house'. Lamb said he joined in with the audience's haranguing so they wouldn't realise that he'd written it.

6 April 1969 The annual Japanese Shinto festival *Kanamara Matsuri*, commonly referred to as the 'Iron Penis Festival', is first held on this date in Kawasaki, Japan. The celebration originates in the legend of a woman who outwits a demon that bites off the penises of her lovers, by hiring a blacksmith to create an iron phallus that breaks the teeth of, and banishes, her infernal tormentor.

18 April 1930 Instead of the usual fifteen-minute news bulletin, the BBC radio service announces that the 'flood of news, official or otherwise, has dried up' and that 'there is no news' to report. Piano music is played for the rest of the slot. Those were the days.

1 July 1936 Salvador Dalí gives a muffled lecture at the first International Surrealism Exhibition in London, while dressed in a full diving suit with brass helmet and holding two dogs on leads in one hand and a billiard cue in the other. As he falls to his knees the audience realise that he's suffocating in the diving helmet. The poet David Gascoyne manages to jimmy it open with a spanner.

4 July 1964 Leicester Hemingway, brother of Ernest, founds the micronation of New Atlantis. The island constitutional republic is a 22sq. m bamboo raft floating off the coast of Jamaica.

8 July 1889 Louis Gustave Binger reveals to the French Geographical Society, Paris, that the Mountains of Kong, a 6000km mountain range stretching across the continent of Africa on European maps, had never actually existed. 'On the horizon, not even a ridge of hills!'

24 July 1904 Final day of the chaotic 1904 Tour de France. The winner, Maurice Garin, is accused of taking the train some of the way.

26 July 1184 Henry VI, King of Germany, holds a *Hoftag* ('informal assembly') in the Petersberg Citadel in Erfurt. The combined weight of the gathered nobles causes the second-storey floor to collapse. All fall into the latrine cesspit below, and sixty of the men drown in liquid excrement.

2 August 2014 Warwickshire man Stuart Kettell pushes a sprout up Mount Snowdon with his nose over four days.

14 August 2017 An Englishman named John Fletcher discovers his 45-year-old pet tortoise Freda lifeless in her pond and spends an hour giving her mouth-to-mouth resuscitation until she returns to life.

9 October 1886 Tchaikovsky writes in his diary: 'I played over the music of that scoundrel Brahms. What a talentless bastard!'

25 October 2019 A team of researchers at the University of Richmond, Virginia, announce that they've successfully taught rats to drive miniature cars as part of a study on mental health.

27 December 2008 The first kiss between robots takes place, between 'Thomas' and 'Janet', during a performance of scenes from *Phantom of the Opera* performed by machines at National Taiwan University of Science and Technology. The robots had caused concern in previous rehearsals when the crew's walkie-talkies interfered with their electronics, causing Thomas and Janet to lunge violently at each other.

IN THE
BEGINNING . . .

The physician and occultist Robert Fludd illustrated the nothingness before Creation in his 1617-1621 work The Metaphysical, Physical, and Technical History of the Two Worlds . . .

The universe was once thought to have started at teatime. In the seventeenth century the archbishop James Ussher (1581-1656) pinpointed the exact date and time of Creation, calculating it to have occurred at 'the entrance of the night preceding the 23rd day of October ... the year before Christ 4004'; so about 6 p.m. on 22 October 4004 BC. This was similar to the estimates of others, including the Venerable Bede (3952 BC), the seventeenth-century astronomer Johannes Kepler (3992 BC) and Sir Isaac Newton, who dated Creation to *c.*4000 BC.

☧✡

The name of the God of the Bible was once believed to be 'Pipi'. The Tetragrammaton is the four-letter name of God in the Hebrew Bible, written and read from right to left and transliterated as YHWH or YHVH, which today is almost universally accepted in the form Yahweh. However, according to the theologian Jerome (*c*.342-420), Greek writers of his time mistook the Hebrew letters for Greek letters, which are read left to right. They therefore took the name of God to be 'Pipi'. [9]

Pronouncing the Tetragrammaton was forbidden to all but the most senior Jewish high priests, but one particular man is recorded as happily breaking this rule to impress. Shabbetai Zevi (1626-1676) was a Sephardic-ordained rabbi who, from the age of twenty, claimed to be the long-awaited Jewish Messiah. This he proved by pronouncing the Tetragrammaton, and also telling his followers that he could fly, but that he couldn't do it for them right now because they weren't worthy of witnessing it. He also married the Torah in a stunt to reinforce his authority. He organised a wedding ceremony between himself and the Scroll of Law that was solemnly performed at Salonika (at the time part of Turkey) sometime between 1653 and 1658. With the holy text dressed up in bridal vestments, the ceremony was conducted before witnesses

9. Not to be confused with Pepi II, the ancient Egyptian pharaoh who came to the throne aged six and is particularly notable (at least in this book) for his habit of having his accompanying servants dipped in honey so that they would attract mosquitoes and other pests away from him.

in the manner of a traditional Jewish wedding. Shabbetai Zevi lovingly placed the ring upon one of the wooden rollers around which the scroll is wound. The groom beamed. The crowd cheered. The rabbis of Salonika banished Zevi from the city.

In Chinese mythology the world was created by the first living being, P'an Ku, a furry horned giant who emerged from a cosmic egg after a wait of 18,000 years. P'an Ku cleaved the egg's shell in two with his axe to form the heavens and Earth, and then fell apart himself. His limbs formed the mountains, his blood the rivers and his breath the wind.

The Kuba people of the Democratic Republic of Congo have the origin myth of the creator god Mbombo, or Bumba, a giant standing alone in darkness and water, who suffered a stomach pain and vomited up the Sun, Moon and stars. The Sun burnt away the waters, revealing the land. Mbombo then threw up nine kinds of animals and, with a final retch, man.

The Big Bang was initially silent, but as soundwaves were produced with the expansion of the universe it rose to a volume of just under 120 decibels, which is about the same as the rock band Deep Purple's legendary 1972 show at London's Rainbow Theatre.[10]

---

10. This decibel level pales in comparison to that of the call of the sperm whale, one of the loudest sounds on the planet, at 230 decibels. (A jet taking off is about 150 decibels.) Anything greater than 200 decibels is loud enough to kill. The deepest note detected in the universe, incidentally, is made by black holes: a B flat 57 octaves lower than middle C, for which you would need a keyboard 15m long to play.

One of the earliest plans to land a man on the Moon was made in seventeenth-century England by Oliver Cromwell's brother-in-law. In 1640, at the age of twenty-six, the theologian Dr John Wilkins (1614-1672) proposed the idea of building a 'Flying Chariot' as 'a conveyance to this other world' and, upon finding inhabitants there, 'to have commerce with them'. The journey to the Moon aboard his contraption of a ship with birdlike wings, powered by springs and gears, would take 180 days, he estimated, and space was unlikely to be uncomfortably cold. Food supplies wouldn't be necessary, as away from the pull of the Earth, which probably extended only 32km up or so, our stomachs would not have food drawn through the digestion system and would remain full. Sadly nothing came of the Jacobean space programme.

In the seventeenth century the English astronomer Sir Paul Neile (1613-1686) made a terrific discovery with his telescope: he'd spotted a giant white elephant on the Moon. He announced his findings, only to be met with public ridicule. It turned out there had been a mouse in his telescope.

In 1838 Reverend Thomas Dick (1774-1857), known as the 'Christian Philosopher', published *Celestial scenery, or, The Wonders of the planetary system displayed*, in which he calculated there to be 21.9 trillion inhabitants in the solar system. He reached the figure by assuming every planet and moon in the system, and even the rings of Saturn, had the same population density as Great Britain at the time. The lunar inhabitants, he stated, made up 4.2 million of this number. Dick's work was massively popular, with Ralph Waldo Emerson among his fans.

Throughout history there have been some magnificent suggestions as to how to attract the attention of alien life. In 1820 the German mathematician Carl Friedrich Gauss (1777-1855) suggested laying out trees to form an enormous geometric proof of the Pythagorean theorem across a large area of Siberian tundra. The shape would be so large that it would be legible to lunar eyes. In 1840 the Austrian astronomer Joseph Johann von Littrow (1781-1840) had the same idea but with a twist, proposing a giant circular canal be dug through the Sahara Desert. Fill this with kerosene, he suggested, and ignite it.

Alien Abduction Insurance was first sold by Florida's Saint Lawrence Insurance Agency in 1987; by 1994, an entity known as the 'UFO Abduction Insurance Company' claimed to have sold a similar policy to 34,000 Americans. Thirty-nine members of the Heaven's Gate cult, who believed they would transform themselves into extra-terrestrial beings, were insured by the London brokerage Goodfellow Rebecca Ingrams Pearson at the cost of $155 annually for a $160,000 pay-out in the event one of their number was abducted by aliens. This included a double-payment indemnity against male members becoming impregnated via 'unknown capabilities of alien technology'. In 1997, as the Hale-Bopp Comet made its closest approach to the Earth, their insurance policies were withdrawn when all were found to have committed suicide in an attempt to ascend to a spacecraft and pursue the comet.

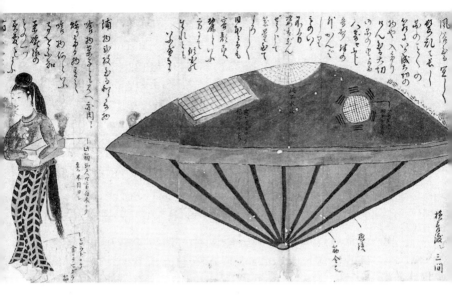

The *Utsuro-bune* ('hollow boat') was a strange alien vessel that Japanese fishermen found off the eastern coast of Japan in 1803, a discovery recorded in multiple contemporary texts. A young woman emerged from the unidentified object, but was unable to speak Japanese. Frightened, the fishermen stuffed her back into her ship and returned it to the sea.

British Rail once patented a flying saucer. British patent office number 1,310,990 was filed by British Rail in 1970, and outlines a design for a nuclear-powered, saucer-shaped transport spaceship,

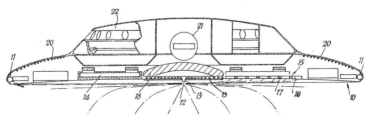

The patent for a space vehicle filed by British Rail in 1970.

designed by Charles Osmond Frederick. What started as a proposal
for a lifting platform had somehow morphed into a large passenger
craft for interplanetary travel, albeit relying on technologies like
laser-based nuclear fusion that were (and are) yet to exist. The patent
was granted in 1973 but lapsed in 1976 due to nonpayment of fees.
Upon the rediscovery of the plans in 2006, a spokesman for the
Department for Transport confirmed to the *Daily Telegraph* that
'we have no plans to introduce nuclear-powered flying saucers to
the network'.

The Apollo 11 lunar module *Eagle* that touched down on the Moon
on 20 July 1969 had noticeably broad foot pads. This design was in
part influenced by the terrifying suggestion made in 1955 by Cornell
scientist Thomas Gold that the Moon's surface could be a thick
layer of light dust that might envelope like quicksand any craft that
landed on it. Even though probes sent as part of NASA's Surveyor
programme suggested a solid surface, Neil Armstrong and Buzz
Aldrin[11] still landed the module on the Moon's surface knowing
that there was a possibility it could swallow them whole.

---

11. Incidentally, Buzz Aldrin's mother's name was Marion Moon.*

   *On a related note, in 2011 an egg-sized meteoroid punched a hole through the roof
   of a house just outside Paris – the family's name? Commette. (For more examples
   of 'nominative determinism' see page 108.)*

   *American humourist Robert Benchley (1889-1945), on being asked why he always
   sat under a sunlamp indoors instead of bathing in the California sunshine, replied:
   'And get hit by a meteor?'

The following is taken from the official NASA transcript of day six of the Apollo 10 mission, which launched on 18 May 1969 as a dry-run test in preparation for the lunar landing of the Apollo 11 mission.

CDR – Commander Thomas P. Stafford
CMP – Command Module Pilot John W. Young
LMP – Lunar Module Pilot Eugène A. Cernan

05 13 29 30 LMP   And what's happening is --

05 13 29 44 CDR   Oh - Who did it?

05 13 29 46 CMP   Who did what?

05 13 29 47 LMP   What?

05 13 29 49 CDR   Who did it? (Laughter)

05 13 29 51 LMP   Where did that come from?

05 13 29 52 CDR   Give me a napkin quick. There's
                  a turd floating through the air.

05 13 29 55 CMP   I didn't do it.
                  It ain't one of mine.

05 13 29 57 LMP   I don't think it's one of mine.

05 13 29 59 CDR   Mine was a little more sticky
                  than that. Throw that away.

05 13 30 06 CMP   God almighty.

05 13 30 08   (Laughter)

05 13 30 10 CDR   What do you see?

05 13 30 12 CMP   Nothing, that's enough for me.

05 13 30 16 LMP   Yes.

05 13 30 18 CMP   Nice going there.

Humans have so far left over 187,400kg of material on the Moon, including:

- A javelin
- A hammer and a feather
- An olive branch made of gold
- A framed family photograph
- A bible
- A pair of tongs
- A television camera
- The ashes of a cremated geologist
- Two golf balls
- Buzz Aldrin's boots
- Four armrests
- Five American flags
- Ninety-six bags of human waste

A 2019 YouGov survey found that 48 per cent of Britons would not want to go to the Moon even if their safety was guaranteed. The top five reasons given were:

'Not interested'
23 PER CENT

'Not enough to see or do on the Moon'
11 PER CENT

'Would rather visit other places on Earth'
10 PER CENT

'No point'
9 PER CENT

'I wouldn't believe you if you guaranteed my safety'
9 PER CENT

'It takes too long to get there'
7 PER CENT

In outer space you develop an instant global consciousness, a people orientation, an intense dissatisfaction with the state of the world, and a compulsion to do something about it. From out there on the Moon, international politics look so petty. You want to grab a politician by the scruff of the neck and drag him a quarter of a million miles out and say, 'Look at that, you son of a bitch.'

Edgar Mitchell (1930-2016), Apollo 14 astronaut

In 2015, having detected an exciting and mysterious intermittent signal on their equipment, Australian astronomers at the Parkes radio telescope eventually traced the source of the interference to the microwave they used to heat their lunch in the observatory kitchen.

The night sky is full of abandoned 'ghost constellations' that you can find on old charts of the sky. The *Telescopium Herschelii* constellation, for example, shown on this 1825 map as the telescope below the Lynx, was established by the astronomer Maximilian Hell (1720-1792) in honour of William Herschel's (1738-1822) discovery of Uranus. It fell out of use before the nineteenth century.

The Earth isn't round; it's fatter at the waist and closer to an oval, or more technically an irregularly shaped ellipsoid. This means it wobbles like a top, which causes its poles to shift naturally several metres each year. In addition to this, between 1993 and 2010 the human race pumped so much water out of the ground (around 2100 gigatonnes) that it affected the shift of the Earth's axis, causing the poles to drift by an additional 80cm.

The Moon has moonquakes, and stars have starquakes. The largest starquake ever detected occurred on 27 December 2004, in the ultracompact stellar corpse SGR 1806-20, about 42,000 light years away. The event released an intense burst of gamma rays equivalent to 1037kW. If this had taken place within ten light years from Earth, all life on our planet would have been incinerated.

If you were to fire a cannon horizontally on the surface of the Moon, with its weaker gravitational pull the cannonball would orbit the entire Moon and it's possible that you'd shoot yourself in the back.

On 13 July 2023 an asteroid the size of a skyscraper narrowly missed Earth, passing closer than the Moon. The worrying part is that scientists didn't notice this until two days *after* it had passed by. Asteroid 2023 NT1 had travelled from the direction of the Sun, which meant telescopes were blinded to it by the solar glare.

It's not just planets that have rings. In 2014, astronomers discovered rings around the asteroid Chariklo. It's unknown why such a small body would have them, but it's thought that perhaps they're collected fragments of a shattered moonlet.

The photons hitting your eye at this moment were flying past Mercury five minutes ago and left the Sun eight minutes ago.

The largest objects in the universe are the Newfound Blobs. Also referred to as Lyman-alpha blobs, several of these enormous blob-like structures composed of hydrogen gas have been spotted since 2000, with some more than 400,000 light years across. They're so far away that their light takes at least 11.5 billion years to reach us. It's thought they're the hearts of young, growing galaxies.

One Venus day (243 Earth days) lasts longer than one Venus year (225 Earth days). In fact, the planet rotates so slowly that you could, theoretically, stroll across its surface and match the speed of the Sun passing through its sky. This means – in the words of astrobiologist David Grinspoon – 'you could watch the sunset forever just by walking.'[12]

Evidence suggests that 3.4 billion years ago there may have been mega-tsunamis on Mars, triggered by colossal landslides falling into an ancient Martian ocean. Waves 120m tall swept boulders the size of buses far inland and flooded more than 570,000 sq. km.

---

12. Should you wish, you can have a Venusian experience on Earth. The Chilean Altiplano in the Atacama Desert has such little protective water vapour in its atmosphere that when standing there you are blasted with the same amount of solar radiation as you would be on Venus.

There are two types of snow on Mars, which both fall only at its coldest points: the poles, in the shadow of cloud cover, and at night. The temperatures are so low that falling water-ice snow sublimates and turns to gas before it reaches the surface, whereas dry-ice snow reaches the ground. It's just deep enough to require snowshoes to cross it, but for skiing you'd have to head to a crater or cliffside where it can build up on a slope.

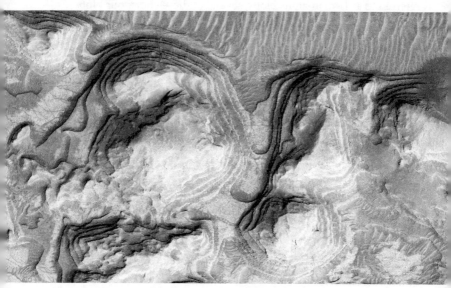

A NASA satellite photo captures the landforms of Arabia Terra, one of the Martian locations thought to have been affected by ancient tsunamis.

Diamonds rain from the sky on Jupiter and Saturn. Lightning storms turn methane into sooty carbon, which hardens into pebbles of graphite that then turn to diamonds. These eventually melt in the liquid sea of the hot cores of the planets. It's also thought likely that these diamond showers could occur on the ice giants Neptune and Uranus, too.

The Jamaican sprinter Usain Bolt could take off on Titan, Saturn's largest moon, according to a calculation made in 2013 by a University of Leicester physics undergraduate named Hannah Lerman. Factoring in Titan's gravity and atmospheric density, if a human wearing a wingsuit managed to hit a speed of 11m per second (Bolt has managed nearly 12m per second on Earth[13]), they would be able to lift off.

One early theory as to the origin of Saturn's rings was proposed in the seventeenth century by the Vatican librarian Leo Allatius (1586-1669), who reportedly wrote an unpublished treatise entitled *De praeputio Domini nostri Jesu Christi Diatriba* ('A Discussion of the Foreskin of Our Lord Jesus Christ'), in which he claimed that the foreskin of the Son of God rose into the heavens and transformed into the rings of Saturn.

Uranus was nearly named George, after King George III. It also has a moon called Margaret – the planet's twenty-seven known moons are all named after characters from the works of William Shakespeare and Alexander Pope.

The origin of the word Neptune is unknown. The scholar Paul Kretschmer (1866-1956) proposed its derivation from the Indo-European *neptu-* ('moist substance'). Thus, Neptune might literally mean 'he who is moist'.

---

13. When Bolt set the world record of 9.69 seconds at the 2008 Summer Olympics, he did it with one shoelace undone.

This advertising poster of the future was produced by NASA/JPL-Caltech in anticipation of the rise of space tourism.

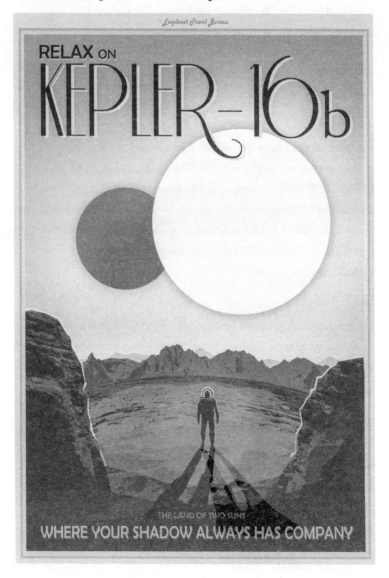

The first close-up images of another world were drawn with crayon. When the Mariner 4 spacecraft flew by Mars on 15 July 1965, it captured the first nearby photographs of another planet. The data was transmitted back to NASA, where the process began to slowly translate the information into a picture. Too impatient to wait, employees at the NASA Jet Propulsion Laboratory printed out the data in strips, taped them together and frantically hand-coloured the assembled pieces to produce this image.

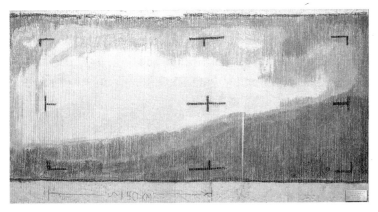

The first close-up images of Mars, taken by the Mariner 4 on 15 July 1965 and hand-coloured by NASA scientists.

It was only in July 2018 that researchers at the University of Cambridge discovered, using data from the European Space Agency's Gaia satellite, that 8-10 billion years ago a dwarf galaxy named the Gaia Sausage collided with the Milky Way. The Sausage was entirely obliterated, while the Milky Way was reshaped through the addition of stars, gas and dark matter, giving our galaxy its distinctive bulge.

What colour is the universe? Actually, it's not far off the colour of this page. Colour code #FFF8E7 is a particular beige that scientists settled on when averaging the light emitted by 200,000 galaxies to form one cosmic spectrum, which, while composed of many different colours, had one overall perceived composite colour. Suggestions for names for this beige included 'skyvory' and 'univeige', but the winner was 'Cosmic latte'.

What does space smell like? The astronaut Don Pettit described a pleasant odour of 'sweet-smelling welding fumes'. Others have compared it to 'burning metal', 'walnuts and brake pads' and 'burnt almond cookie'. Buzz Aldrin and Neil Armstrong described it as like gunpowder.

Sniffing a comet would be a less pleasant experience. In 2014 data from the spectrometer aboard the European Space Agency's Rosetta probe revealed that the comet 67P/Churyumov-Gerasimenko possessed a rather sassy fragrance of rotten eggs, cat urine and bitter almonds. 'It's really fabulous', explained Kathrin Altwegg of the University of Bern, Switzerland.

What does space taste like? In 2009 astronomers at the Institut de radioastronomie millimétrique telescope in Spain used spectroscopy to study a vast dust cloud at the centre of the Milky Way known as Sagittarius B2. It turned out to be composed mostly of alcohol – specifically a blend of methanol, ethanol and other ingredients including ethyl formate, an organic molecule that smells of strong spirit and tastes like raspberries.

It's impossible for astronauts to whistle while they work. The air pressure in a space suit is only 3 newtons per sq. cm, whereas normal atmospheric pressure is 10 newtons per sq. cm. This means there are not enough air molecules to blow with your lips to make the sound.

Statistically one of the biggest dangers in space is drowning. The most recent near-fatal incident in space occurred on 16 July 2013 when Luca Parmitano, the first Italian to walk in space, took a spacewalk with fellow astronaut Christopher Cassidy around the International Space Station (ISS). Parmitano reported feeling water on the back of his neck inside his suit, and his helmet began to fill rapidly with water. He watched helplessly as it floated into his eyes, nose and mouth. Cassidy dragged him back into the ISS, and they quickly removed his helmet and gloves. It was later found that about a litre of water had leaked from his coolant system into the spacesuit, and if he hadn't removed his helmet in time he would have drowned. 'He looks fine,' Cassidy radioed NASA, before correcting: 'He looks miserable, but okay.' Astronauts on the ISS are also at risk of drowning in their own exhaled breath; they have to sleep beside fans that keep the surrounding air clear.

Neutron stars are so densely packed with neutrons that a teaspoonful of their material weighs more than a trillion kilograms – to achieve a comparable density with people, you would have to squeeze every human on Earth together into a space the size of a sugar cube.

In the past, cosmonauts have gone into space armed. This is the TP-82, an out-of-service, triple-barrelled pistol issued to Soviet cosmonauts on space missions. Landing in the Russian tundra presented potential survival risks, so the TP-82 was designed to help defend against predators and send up distress signals, with a machete hidden in the buttstock.

The Sun loses 4 million tonnes of mass per second due to fusion converting its mass to energy. In the 4.5 billion years of its lifespan so far, the Sun has lost a total of about 10^{24} tonnes of material – which is more than 100 times the mass of the Earth.

The Sun isn't yellow, it's white –
with a touch of turquoise.

Athanasius Kircher's (1601-1680) map of the Sun from 1665 is full of mistaken beliefs about our star, including mountain ranges at its poles and a swirling blue sea taking up much of its surface. Kircher based the wonderfully strange map on the observations of sunspots made by the German Jesuit Christoph Scheiner (1573-1650), who believed that sunspots were satellites of the Sun.

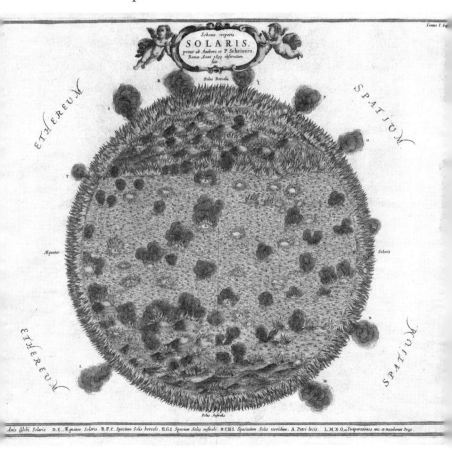

In 2017 the hottest point in the solar system was, for a brief moment, a site just north of the English town of Didcot, which a few months earlier had been voted Britain's 'most normal town' in a national poll. As part of a nuclear fusion energy project at a private lab run by Tokamak Energy, researchers achieved plasma temperatures of over 15 million °C, which is hotter than the centre of the Sun.

In 1995 the coldest place in the universe was, briefly, Cambridge, Mass, in a laboratory at the Massachusetts Institute of Technology. A team led by German physicist Wolfgang Ketterle cooled sodium gas to half-a-billionth of a degree above absolute zero (-273.15°C). By comparison the Moon is a positively cosy -247°C. This record for lowest temperature still stands.

The earliest named author in history was a woman named Enheduanna (c.2285-2250BC), an ancient Sumerian lunar priestess. Today she is remembered for the poetry and hymns she composed relating details of her life, particularly the 153-line work *Nin-me-šara* ('The Exaltation of Inanna'), which features her lunar observations as priestess to the Moon goddess Nanna. She lived 1500 years before Homer, 1700 years before Sappho and 2000 years before Aristotle.

The oldest 'book' in the British Library is made of bone, etched sometime between 1600BC and 1050BC. 'Oracle bones' are animal bones, often from oxen and turtles, heated until cracks were formed; these were then deciphered by fortune-tellers, who used them to answer questions ranging from the future weather to the outcomes of military campaigns. Sometimes the oracle bones were also carved with records of astronomical occurrences. The bones are quite rare, partly because when discovered they were often mistaken for dragon bones which, according to tradition, could be ground up for medicinal purposes. They were often reburied or sometimes eaten.

The longest work ever written was commissioned by the Yongle Emperor of China's Ming dynasty. The *Yongle Encyclopaedia* or *Yongle Dadian* ('Great Canon of Yongle') is a mostly lost Chinese encyclopaedia that incorporated all recorded knowledge for the convenience of its imperial reader. Work began in 1403. An initial team of 100 scholars grew into an army of 2169, who travelled across China to find written works to feed into the omnivorous project. Some 8000 texts on every subject were absorbed, and when the project was completed five years later, in 1408, the encyclopaedia comprised 22,937 manuscript rolls bearing some 370 million Chinese handwritten characters. The complete encyclopaedia would have occupied roughly 40 cubic metres of space – the same volume as a modern 11m lorry trailer.

There is a book so long that it could destroy the universe. Theoretically, the record of the longest work could be claimed by printing the work *Googolplex Written Out*, published online in multiple PDF volumes by Wolfgang H. Nitsche in 2013, in which the number googolplex (1 followed by 10^{100} zeros) is typed out in full. Before clicking 'Add to cart' for a hard copy, though, it's worth considering that in doing so you would be obliterating all known existence. Printing all the zeros of a googolplex would require 10^{94} books. If each of these books had a mass of 100g, then the total mass of the set would be 10^{93}kg. This is not only greater than the mass of the Earth, but also the mass of the entire Milky Way Galaxy.

The maximum possible size of a page of a PDF file is 381 × 381km.

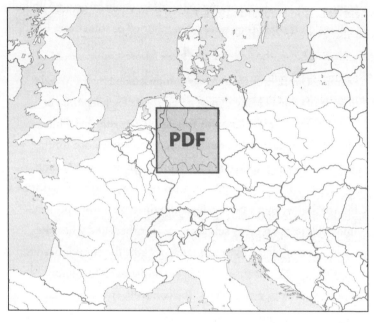

Top five Google autofill search results for 🔍 'how do I convert to ...'

🔍 how do I convert to **islam**

🔍 how do I convert to **judaism**

🔍 how do I convert to **catholicism**

🔍 how do I convert to **pdf**

🔍 how do I convert to **buddhism**

In the West the record for most published works by one author is held by L. Ron Hubbard (1911-1986), founder of Scientology, who also wrote one of (this) world's longest novels. The ten-volume story *Mission Earth*, the first volume of which was published in 1985, runs to 1.2 million words across 3992 pages. Critics were not favourable, and the book was even banned in places like Dalton, Georgia, where it was decried as 'anti-social, perverted and anti-everything'.

Hubbard produced an astounding 1084 published works in his lifetime. His most curious work by far, though, is *Excalibur*, which reportedly came to him while having a reaction to nitrous oxide during a dental procedure in 1938. He claimed the book would be 'somewhat more important, and would have a greater impact upon people, than the Bible'. Though it was never published, Hubbard briefly advertised a very limited edition for $1500 per copy in 1957, with the warning that 'four of the first fifteen people who read it went insane'. He told his literary agent, Forrest J. Ackerman, that when he'd sent the manuscript to a New York publisher the reader had jumped out of the skyscraper window. It was this book that formed the basis for his later infamous work *Dianetics* (1950).

The romance novelist Barbara Cartland (1901-2000) holds the record for most published works in one year, producing twenty-three in 1976. Just as remarkably, in her youth she invented the first long-range, aircraft-towed glider, which in 1931 resulted in a glider flight of 320km, smashing previous records. She was awarded the Bishop Wright Air Industry Award at Kennedy Airport, USA, in 1984 for her contribution to the development of aviation.

In 2016 it was discovered that Anne Frank's (1929-1945) diary has two secret pages of dirty jokes, hidden behind a layer of pasted brown paper. Using digital image-processing, Dutch researchers were able to read them. 'I'll use this spoiled page to write down "dirty" jokes,' Frank wrote. 'A man had a very ugly wife, and he didn't want to have relations with her. One evening he came home and then he saw his friend in bed with his wife, and the man said: "He gets to, and I have to!!!"' She then writes about prostitutes: 'Women like that accost [men] on the street and then they go together. In Paris they have big houses for that,' she writes, adding 'Papa has been there.'

Edward Elgar's 'Dorabella cypher'.

The unsolved 'Dorabella cypher', written by the married composer Edward Elgar (1857-1934) in 1897 to Dora Penny, a family friend seventeen years his junior, has never been broken. It's possible that it's not even a text at all but a melody, the eight different positions of the semicircles, rotating clockwise, matching the notes of the scale. Some have confidently claimed to have cracked the code but often provide a message even more nonsensical; see that of Tim S. Roberts of Central Queensland University, for example: 'P.S. Now droop beige weeds set in it – pure idiocy – one entire bed! Luigi Ccibunud lovingly tuned liuto studio two.'

The average person has thirteen secrets, according to a 2017 paper by Michael L. Slepian and Katharine H. Greenaway published in the *Journal of Personality and Social Psychology*, which examined 10,055 secrets across ten different studies. The same study also found that people preoccupied with secrets can feel physically weighed down by them and tend to judge hills as steeper and distances longer than they actually are.

Donald Trump had his Twitter (now known as 'X') account hacked by a Dutchman who guessed his password to be 'yourefired', his catchphrase from his television show *The Apprentice*. The same hacker took over his account again two years later by guessing the new password as 'maga2020!'.

In 2013 it was revealed during a UK court case that journalists had hacked the phone of British footballer Wayne Rooney by guessing his password as 'Stella Artois'.

Nuclear Code 00000000 – for fifteen years the code to electronically 'unlock' the US arsenal of strategic nuclear missiles, which sit ready to launch in silos across the USA, was '00000000'. This remained in place from 1962 to 1977, until a Minuteman missile launch control officer named Bruce Blair alerted his superiors and members of Congress to the dangers of the easily crackable code, and the US Air Force finally changed them.

A royal list of daily passwords 'for the court' and 'for the city' signed at the head by Queen Anne, February 1704. These lists were circulated to the guards at the gates of the City of London.

T. Lobsang Rampa was a Tibetan monk who wrote a global bestseller called *The Third Eye* in 1956, until his secret was revealed: he was actually Cyril Henry Hoskin, the son of an English plumber from Plympton. Confronted, Hoskin explained that the soul of Lobsang Rampa had taken over his body after he fell out of a fir tree in Thames Ditton while trying to take a photograph of an owl.

SOME PEN NAMES OF THE COMPULSIVELY PSEUDONYMOUS

Jonathan Swift (1667-1745) *Countess of Fizzlerumpf; Dr Andrew Tripe; Lemuel Gulliver; Isaac Bickerstaff; M. B. Drapier; a shoeboy; Gregory Miso-sarum; Simon Wagstaff; T. Fribble; T. N. Philomath; Jack Frenchman; M'Flor O'Squarr*

Daniel Defoe (1660-1731) *Eye Witness; T. Taylor; Andrew Morton, merchant; Betty Blueskin; Boatswain Trinkolo; Count Kidney Face; Sir Fopling Tittle-Tattle; Heliostrapolis, secretary to the Emperor of the Moon (among some 200 other pen names)*

Anton Chekhov (1860-1904) *Antosha Chekhonte; Man Without Spleen; My Brother's Brother; Doctor Without Patients; Nut #6; The Prosaic Poet; Shileer Shakespearevich Goethe; Champagne; Haika No. 6; Haika No. 9; Grach; Akaki Tarantulov; Archip Indian; Vasily Spiridonov Svolachev; Someone*

Benjamin Franklin (1706-1790) *Caelia Shortface; Martha Careful; Busy Body; Anthony Afterwit; Alice Addertongue; Richard Saunders; Polly Baker; Silence Dogood*

L. Ron Hubbard (1911-1986) *Bernard Hubbel; Legionnaire 14830; Kurt von Rachen; René Lafayette; Joe Blitz; Winchester Remington Colt, Lt Scott Morgan; Barry Randolph; Capt Humbert Reynolds*

Hapax legomenon is the term for a word that occurs only once in
a written work, or indeed the total works of an author. The rather
beautiful word 'flother', for example, a synonym for snowflake, is
historically found only once in written English in a manuscript called
The XI Pains of Hell (*c*.1275). *Honorificabilitudinitatibus*, the plural
of the medieval Latin word *honōrificābilitūdinitās* ('the state of being
able to achieve honours') is a *hapax legomenon* of Shakespeare's
works. In Genesis 6:14, when Noah receives his instructions from
God to build the Ark, he is told to build it out of *gofer* (translated as
'gopher wood'), a mysterious word that doesn't appear anywhere
else in the Bible nor the Hebrew language. The words 'girl' and 'boy'
also occur only once in the Bible. Only one 'burp' features in the
works of Shakespeare, and it's emitted by Sir Toby Belch in *Twelfth
Night*. The word 'she' occurs only once in *The Hobbit*.

When Gustave Doré's (1832-1883) publisher refused to take the
risk of publishing the illustrator's collection of 135 illustrations
for Dante's *Inferno* in 1861, Doré did it himself. In just two weeks
the book had sold out, and he received a telegram from the same
publisher: 'Success! Come quickly! I am an ass!'

The largest surviving medieval manuscript in Europe was
supposedly created with the assistance of the Devil. According to
legend, in the early thirteenth century in the Benedictine monastery
of Podlažice in Bohemia, a scribe known as Herman the Recluse
was condemned to be immured (sealed up behind a wall while still
alive) for breaking his vows. After pleading for his life, Herman was
spared by the abbot on the rather unfair condition that the monk

write down all of humanity's knowledge in one night. Herman wrote frantically but at midnight he admitted defeat, and in desperation prayed for help from the Devil. By morning, Lucifer had completed the beautifully illuminated work known as the *Codex Gigas*, and in thanks Herman included in the book a full-page portrait of the Prince of Darkness. The book now resides at the National Library of Sweden in Stockholm.

The world's shortest published poem is this four-legged m, written by the Armenian-American poet Aram Saroyan in the 1960s. What exactly it means is unclear. As the m and the n appear to be in the process of dividing like a cell, the mathematical poet and critic Bob Grumman called it 'a close-up of an alphabet being born'. Saroyan has form in this area, having knocked out the one-word poem 'Lighght' in 1965, which went on to be known as 'the most expensive word in history'. 'Lighght' earned Saroyan a $500 cash award from the National Endowment for the Arts and kicked off a national debate in America over the waste of public money. 'If my kid came home from school spelling like that,' one congressman said, 'I would have stood him in the corner with a dunce cap.' Ronald Reagan was still making sarcastic allusions to 'lighght' twenty-five years later. 'I got intrigued by the look of individual words,' shrugged Saroyan. 'The word "guarantee", for instance, looks to me a bit like a South American insect.'

 In terms of theatrical brevity, one of the shortest plays ever staged is *The Exile* by the French playwright Tristan Bernard (1866-1947). The curtain is raised to reveal the setting: a mountain cabin near the frontier, in which the Mountaineer sits beside a fire. There is a knock on the door, and the Exile enters the room. The entire play is the following exchange:

EXILE: Whoever you are, have pity on a hunted man.
    There is a price on my head.
MOUNTAINEER: How much?

Curtain.

The *Liber Linteus Zagrabiensis* is a manuscript found wrapped around a mummy. In 1848 a junior Croatian bureaucrat named Mihajlo Baric bought as a souvenir in Alexandria a mummified female corpse housed in a large sarcophagus. On his return to Vienna, Baric put the mummy on display in the corner of his living room and removed its linen wrappings for display in a separate cabinet. There the mummy stood until 1859, when Baric died. It wasn't until 1891 that it was realised that the strips of bandage were covered in Etruscan text and could be reassembled to form a semi-complete manuscript. Dated to *c.*250 BC, the *Liber Linteus Zagrabiensis* had started out as a canvas about 3.4m wide, which was then folded into twelve pages and used as writing material with black and red ink. The Etruscan language has not yet been fully deciphered, but among the 1200 legible words of the manuscript are recognisable dates and names of gods that suggest the text is a religious calendar, which from Roman examples we know were used to record religious ceremonies and rituals. From a scrap of papyrus that accompanied the corpse, her provenance was deciphered: she was an Egyptian named Nesi-hensu, wife of Paher-hensu, a tailor from Thebes. She had died at a time when mummification of the deceased was just becoming a popular technique, and linen for it was in such high demand that there was a severe shortage. Egyptians turned to whatever they could get their hands on, shredding clothes, sails and even manuscripts imported by foreign traders.

King Tutankhamun (*fl.*1400-1301 BC) was laid to rest with his penis mummified at a ninety-degree angle, with a scarab in place of his heart. He also appears to have been doused in an inky black oil before being placed inside his sarcophagus, with evidence suggesting that this then caused him to spontaneously combust. It's thought that these embalming features may have been an attempt to make him resemble Osiris, god of the underworld.[14] Among the treasures in his tomb were a collection of boomerangs, which the ancient Egyptians used for hunting waterfowl; the earliest example of a folding 'Z-bed'; and a knife made from a metal that was only recently confirmed as being iron from a meteorite. He was also provided with 145 soiled loin cloths for use as underwear in the afterlife.

The oldest mummified human remains were discovered not in Egypt as one might expect, but in the 8000-year-old graves of the Sado Valley, southern Portugal.

---

14. Unique burial features continue to be discovered. In 2022 at the Quweisna necropolis in the Nile delta, archaeologists uncovered several mummies, dating to *c.* 640-300 BC, with replacement tongues made of gold. The theory is that these were intended to aid the deceased in speaking to Osiris, who was also known as the 'Lord of Silence' after his hatred of noise.

Creme Puff was the oldest domestic cat that has ever lived, dying in 2005 at the age of thirty-eight years and three days. Her owner said her age was due to the 'eyedropper full of red wine' he gave her every two days.

When the Aztec Empire was founded in 1427,
Oxford University was at least 330 years old.

When Harvard University was founded in 1636,
Galileo was still alive – he was seventy-one years old.

SOME ADVICE FOR A LONG LIFE

THE INVENTOR OF VASELINE, Robert Chesebrough (1837-1933), was so convinced of its health benefits that he ate a spoonful of the substance every day of his life. During a serious attack of pleurisy in his mid-fifties, he had his nurse rub him from head to foot with Vaseline. He died at the age of ninety-six at his house in Spring Lake, New Jersey.

JEANNE CALMENT (1875-1997) of France lived to an age of 122 years and 164 days. The oldest documented person to have ever lived, she outlived both her daughter and grandson. She claimed to have met Vincent Van Gogh ('ugly', 'very disagreeable', 'reeked of alcohol'), ate 1kg of chocolate a week, drank port and smoked until the age of 117. She attributed her longevity to a diet rich in olive oil.

SCOTSWOMAN CATHY HILLOCK celebrated her 102nd birthday in July 2022 and credited staying single and never marrying as the secret to her long life.

MARY FLIP OF ARIZONA attributes her 102 years to her love of tequila; while fellow America Andrew E. Slavonic credits his 104 years to drinking Coors beer daily without fail.

THE ITALIAN SUPERCENTENARIAN Emma Martina Luigia Morano had been the world's oldest person for nearly a year when she died at the age of 117, on 15 April 2017. She had seen ninety Italian governments come and go, and said the secret was raw eggs, chocolate and thinking positively.

WILBUR GLENN VOLIVA (1870-1942), the American evangelist and controller of the town of Zion, Illinois, was a loud believer in the Flat Earth theory and that he would live to the age of 120 due to his diet of Brazil nuts and buttermilk. He died at the age of seventy-two, shortly after it was discovered that he had embezzled millions of town funds. He was deposed, fell into personal bankruptcy and was forced by the town's new administrators to put a sticker on his car displaying a spherical Earth.[15]

15. Zion, which is 64km north of Chicago, has a fascinating history. Established in 1901 by the faith healer John Alexander Dowie (1847-1907), the entire town was built in the shape of the Union Jack flag, with every street named after a figure of the Bible. Almost every enjoyable feature of daily life of the outside world was banned – this included gambling, dancing, baseball and football, swearing, spitting, theatres, circuses, alcohol, pool, pork, oysters, medicine and doctors, politicians and, for some reason, tan-coloured shoes. Zion police officers each carried a billy club in one holster and a Bible in another, and their helmets were painted with a dove and the word PATIENCE. Anyone caught smoking was branded a 'STINKPOT' and punished. Zion was the first place in the world to have anti-smoking billboards.

When the Egyptian pyramids were built, woolly mammoths were still alive. Most had died out *c*.10,500 years ago, but some were trapped by rising sea levels on Wrangel Island, Russia, and roamed there until their extinction *c*.3700 years ago.

The vending machine is almost 2000 years old – the first known example was invented by Hero of Alexandria (*fl.*AD 60) to dispense holy water when a coin was inserted into a slot. Hero is also credited with inventing the first steam engine, the thermometer, the force pump that would later be used in fire engines, and a self-filling wine bowl.

In June 2023 all South Koreans become younger by at least one year, when two traditional age-counting methods were scrapped and replaced with international standards. One of the old methods included time spent in the womb, while the other considered a person zero at birth and added a year on 1 January. As of 28 June 2023, with the introduction of international standards, a person born on 29 June 2003 is nineteen under the international system, twenty under the counting-age system and twenty-one under the 'Korean age' system.

Several court physicians of ancient Egypt held the job title of 'Shepherd of the Royal Anus' (*neru pehut*), which can also be translated as 'Herdsman of the Anus' or 'Guardian of the Anus'. This was part of the Egyptian system of each of royal doctors specialising in treating only one illness or body part – there was also a Royal Keeper of the Pharaoh's Left Eye and a Royal Keeper of the Pharaoh's Right Eye.

Bald's Leechbook (*c.*925-955) is a manuscript in the British Library
with recipes taken from Greek and Roman authors, as well as from
Anglo-Saxon physicians with names like 'Oxa' and 'Dun'. Though the
majority of its potions and rudimentary treatments should be safely
consigned to history (like treating cataracts with raw hare's liver), in
2015 Christina Lee, a professor in Viking studies at the University
of Nottingham, translated the recipe for an eye salve involving
garlic, leeks, wine and cow bile, and tested its antibiotic effects on
the notoriously resistant 'superbug' bacterium Meticillin-resistant
Staphylococcus Aureus. To the team's astonishment, they found that
the Anglo-Saxon remedy succeeded in destroying much of the bug
that modern antibiotics fail to treat.

'Mouse rotted and given to children to eat, remedieth pissing the
bed,' advises John Partridge in *The Widow's Treasure* (1595), which
also contains the advice to steam your clothes with boiling mercury
to get rid of lice (and with them, your higher brain function).

In the seventeenth-century recipe collection of Anna Maria Luisa
de' Medici (1667-1743) can be found a potion for treating infant
convulsions using the pulverised skull of a man who died violently
but was not buried. To prevent strokes and improve blood flow,
drink female rhinoceros blood; or vaginally insert St Ignatius beans
'to lower the monster of women'. (Considering the beans contain the
deadly alkaloids strychnine and brucine this would certainly have
had a potent effect, but probably not the desired outcome.)

To jolt the comatose awake, the French physician Bernard de Gordon (*c.*1258-1318) recommended full-throated screaming at the patient, or the loud playing of musical instruments by their head or holding squealing pigs in their face. If all else fails, pluck their chest hairs.

The British neuroscientist Adrian Owen studied the phenomenon of awareness in coma patients and was told the story of a girl in a vegetative state whose mother would visit every day and play her favourite Celine Dion album on repeat. After several months she became one of the few people to recover from this state. Her first words to her mother upon waking were: 'If I ever hear that Celine Dion album again, I will kill you.'

You shed about 35kg of skin in your lifetime, according to a 2011 study published in *Environmental Science & Technology*. The researchers also found that the squalene oil in the shedded skin reacts with harmful ozone, so skin dust technically improves the air quality of your home.

William Harvey's 1628 study of the human circulatory system inspired others to test his findings, including Sir Christopher Wren, who dissolved opium in wine and injected it into the vein of a dog. In 1666 the physician Richard Lower injected soup into the veins of dogs to see if this would feed them; and later transfused blood from a lamb into a volunteered lunatic named Arthur Coga in order to calm the man's brain which was 'a little too warm'.

This analogical diagram from the Jewish rabbi-physician Tobias Cohen's *Ma'aseh Tuviyah* (1708) compares the workings of the human body to the functions of a house: the heart being the master's residence, the stomach is the kitchen, and the digestive tract leads to plumbing of sewage tanks and waterworks. It's thought that the diagram was intended to serve as a mnemonic device, to help student physicians to memorise anatomical details.

On average you swallow about 1.5 litres of phlegm every day, and you'll cry about 64 litres of tears in your lifetime.

You can't bite your own finger off. A 2012 study by the Ilmenau University of Technology looking at hand injuries caused by electric car windows showed that an average of 1485 newtons of force was needed to merely fracture a human finger. This is twice the amount of force than that of the hardest bite you can make, and about ten times the force exerted when you chew normally. Your best bet would be gnawing at the knuckle for an extended period.

There is gold in humans. A body weighing 70kg will on average contain a total amount of about 0.2mg of gold, or 10 nanolitres in purified form. This would form a gold cube with sides of 0.22mm, but before you go eying up your friends be aware that this is worth about twenty pence. Gold's function in the human body was always a mystery until it was recently established as being instrumental in the transmission of electrical signals through the body.[16]

---

16. Gold can be found in other unexpected places – it literally grows on trees, for example. Australian scientists have found that gum (*Eucalyptus*) leaves contain gold, drawn up by their roots that can grow 40m downward in search of water. The Sun contains almost 2.5 trillion tonnes of gold, which is more than enough to fill Earth's oceans, even though that's just eight atoms of gold for every trillion atoms of hydrogen – a comparatively tiny amount to the mass of the Sun.*

There is more gold in one tonne of personal computers than there is in 17 tonnes of gold ore.

*In 2016 researchers discovered that the Swiss collectively flush around 3 tonnes of silver and 43kg of gold in effluent and sludge from wastewater treatment plants annually, amounting to about 3 million Swiss francs ($3.1 million).

The human body contains around 1g of silicon, an element
that is often found together with gold in nature, but its metabolic
function is currently unknown.

The phrase 'blowing smoke up your arse' originates in an actual
medical procedure in Europe, believed to be an effective method
for resuscitating the drowned. One of the first documented cases
of the 'procedure' involved a sailor recommending to a husband of a
seemingly drowned woman that he insert the stem of his lit smoking
pipe up her backside, cover the pipe's bowl with perforated paper,
and blow. This apparently revived the woman, and tobacco smoke
enemas became thought of as a potent resuscitation technique.

In the 1780s England's Royal Humane Society even installed smoke
enema resuscitation kits at locations along the river Thames (where
today you find buoyant life rings instead). By the nineteenth century
the enemas were an established restorative treatment for drowning,
and a wide range of ailments as well, until the surgeon Sir Benjamin
Brodie (1783-1862) conclusively put a stop to it in 1811.[17]

SOS is not an acronym; it doesn't stand for 'save our souls', nor anything
else. It was just thought that the Morse code signal of '. . .---. . .' would
be easy to remember. Incidentally, Wi-Fi doesn't stand for anything,
either. It was simply catchier than 'IEEE 802.11b Direct Sequence'.

---

17. In 2021 Dr Takanori Takebe of the Tokyo Medical and Dental University published
a study in which air-deprived mice and pigs were saved with enemas of oxygenated
liquid, suggesting that one day we might develop the technology to allow humans to
breathe through our anuses.

During the Battle of Shiloh fought on 6-7 April 1862 in the American Civil War, cases were reported of injured soldiers with wounds that glowed in the dark. It's thought that this is evidence of infection by *Photorhabdus luminescens*, a bacterium that is bioluminescent for reasons not yet understood. The bacterium also has an antibiotic effect, contributing to the survival rate of infected soldiers, and leading to the glowing wound phenomenon being nicknamed 'Angel's Glow'.

If you inhale a pea seed, it can grow into a pea plant in your lung.

About 150 cases of leprosy are reported in the US each year. One-fifth of those cases are reported in Florida.

Rock squirrels in the Grand Canyon carry the Black Plague.

Since 2022, doctors in Canada have been prescribing memberships of national parks to patients.

In early twentieth-century America the scam artist John Romulus Brinkley (1885-1942) amassed millions of dollars from his patented panacea for male ailments, which he performed surgically despite possessing zero medical qualifications. This widely touted, and scarcely believable, treatment consisted of transplanting goat testicles into the human patient's testicular sac, where the foreign gland would usually just be absorbed by the body. The 'goat-gland doctor' found international fame and great wealth, until word spread that patients were dying from infections, and he was finally banned from practising medicine. He died penniless, after lawsuits had stripped him of every ill-gotten dollar.[18]

The Elizabethan 'pigeon slippers' cure involved cutting open two of the birds and attaching them to the feet of the patient, a treatment that stemmed from the belief in the dove as a messenger of the afterlife. Catherine of Braganza, wife of Charles II, was given the treatment by her desperate Portuguese palace medics but died nevertheless on 31 December 1705.

A 2016 paper published in *Neuroscience Letters* entitled 'The influence of dental occlusion on the body balance in unstable platform increases after high intensity exercise' showed that straightening people's teeth also improved their posture and body-balance ability.

---

18. Brinkley's testicular treatment has a precursor in the work of the Mauritian physiologist Charles-Édouard Brown-Séquard (1817-1894), who at the age of seventy-two reported 'rejuvenated sexual prowess' after performing 'subcutaneous injection of extracts of monkey testis' on himself. (He had the reputation of an eccentric ever since he swallowed the vomit of a cholera patient during an outbreak in 1853 in order to contract the disease himself and find a cure.) He further claimed, at a meeting of the Société de biologie in Paris, that a hypodermic injection of a fluid sourced from guinea pig testicles resulted in rejuvenation and could prolong human life. 'The lecture must be seen as further proof of the necessity of retiring professors who have attained their threescore and ten years,' wrote a journalist for one Vienna medical publication.*

   *And if only to complete a pair of testicular footnotes to hang at the bottom of this page, it should be noted that the potency of testicles has been respected since antiquity. Pliny the Elder (23/24-79) recommends athletes chew lamb testicles before a race for a boost, while the ancient Assyrians enshrined the protection of men's testicles from women into law.

In the Middle Ages physicians known as 'piss prophets' diagnosed illnesses by examining, smelling and cheerfully tasting the urine of the patient, consulting works like Theophilus Protospatharius's seventh-century text *De Urinis*, or *Fasciculus Medicinae* (1491), illustrations from which are shown here. The coloured urine wheels helped to advise the diagnosis.

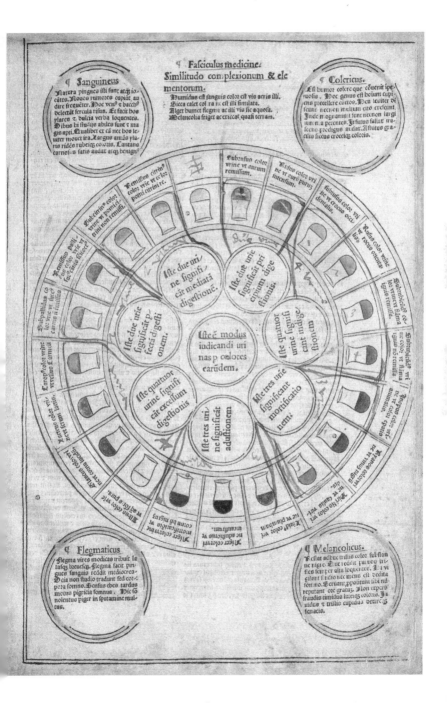

♀♂

James Graham (1745-94) was a notorious quack of eighteenth-century London, who opened his Temple of Health in Pall Mall, London, in 1780. On stepping into the entrance hall of the Temple, visitors passed piles of walking sticks, crutches, eyeglasses and ear trumpets that they were told had been discarded by previous customers cured by Graham's treatments. The grand feature of the Temple was Graham's magnificent mechanical 'celestial bed' that couples wishing to conceive could rent for an hour. Standing on forty pillars of coloured glass 'of the most exquisite workmanship', the bed had mechanisms that routinely sprayed perfumes of flowers and spices, and various magnets and electrical machines that caused it to hum, electrified with a restorative charge. With its adjustable frame, the bed could be set at various angles, and automata moved about it as music played, reportedly matching the tempo to the exercise of those between its sheets. Conception was guaranteed.[19]

♀♂

In Fiji there is a tradition for the young man to present the father of his beloved with a whale's tooth before asking for the hand of his daughter in marriage. The challenge with this is that the tooth has to be freshly wrenched from a living whale's mouth.

♀♂

In traditional Hindu Balinese society, young men and women undergo a ritual tooth-filing ceremony, shaving down six of their teeth in order to advertise their arrival at marrying age.

---

19. No such promises were made for another curious bedded couple in Paris in 1187, when Richard I of England and Philip II of France spent the night together in the same bed to symbolically cement their alliance – 'political, not sexual', emphasises the *Oxford Dictionary of National Biography*.

'Resusci Anne' is the name of the silicon dummy torso that has been used to train hundreds of millions of people in the technique of cardiopulmonary resuscitation (CPR). It was invented in 1960 by the Norwegian toy designer Asmund Laerdal (1913-1981), who based the face on a plaster death mask (shown here) popular with artists that was known as the Inconnue de la Seine (The Unknown Woman of the Seine). This was said to be of an unidentified young woman found drowned in the River Seine in Paris in the late 1880s. Her body was exhibited at the Paris mortuary, where the morgue pathologist was so struck by her beauty and enigmatic smile that he had a plaster cast made of her face.

George Washington (1732-1799) wore sets of dentures made from the teeth of enslaved people and cows, as well as ivory of walrus, elephant and hippopotamus.

When Abraham Lincoln (1809-1865) went to have a tooth pulled without any anaesthesia, the dentist accidentally snapped off a piece of his jawbone.

George W. Bush and Stephen Spielberg are among a small section of the population that have a distinctive diagonal ear lobe crease (DELC), known as 'Frank's sign' after the physician Dr Sander T. Frank who noticed that it seems to indicate a greater risk for coronary artery disease (CAD), which can cause heart attacks. No one knows why this is. Sculptures of the Roman Emperor Hadrian (76-138) show him with the earlobe crease, and it's believed that he did indeed die from CAD and heart failure.

Some of the earliest subjects in the development of the medical science of endoscopy and oesophagoscopy in the nineteenth century were sword-swallowers. In the 1850s, physicians looking for volunteers to test the rigid oesophagoscope, a new tool inserted down the throat to examine the upper digestive tract, saw that most people found it impossible not to gag and choke on the instrument. Adolf Kussmaul (1822-1902), an enterprising physician of Freiburg, Germany, had noticed the skill in which local sword-swallowers controlled their posture and gag reflex, and hired them to test the pioneering airway endoscopy tools that are still used today around the world in more flexible and advanced form. Hundreds of millions of patients have benefited from the physician and performers' early work, which also aided in the development of the X-ray, fluoroscopy and electrocardiograms.

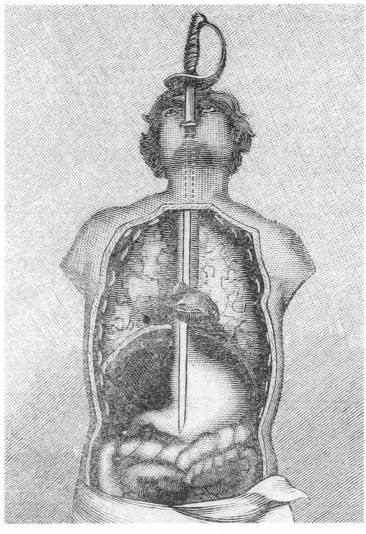

'Position occupied by the sword blade in the body', from Magic: Stage Illusions and Scientific Diversions *(1897).*

A demonstration of the forgotten 'science' of metoposcopie, the study of forehead lines to determine character. From *Physiognomie and chiromancie, metoposcopie, the symmetrical proportions and signal moles of the body …* (1653) by Richard Saunders.

On 27 January 1851 Dr George Merryweather, curator of the Whitby Literary and Philosophical Society's Museum, gave a three-hour address to members of the society announcing his invention, the Tempest Prognosticator, or 'The Leech Barometer'. Merryweather claimed that his device predicted weather by using leeches, which when disturbed by an impending storm would climb the glass chamber of his device and ring a bell at the top. He lobbied the British government to invest in his design and put it to use around the British coasts, but they opted instead for the more traditional science of Robert FitzRoy's storm glass.

The Swedish writer August Strindberg (1849-1912) conducted experiments based on his own amateur scientific theories. One of these was the idea that plants had nervous systems. He was caught by a policeman injecting low-hanging apples with morphine, but after he explained his theory it was decided that he wasn't a fruit poisoner, and he was released.

Every day for thirty years the Venetian physiologist Santorio Santorio (1561-1636) routinely ate, worked and slept on a giant weighing-chair set of scales, recording his every ingestion and excretion to study the fluctuations of his body weight against his solid and liquid waste. In doing so he originated the study of the metabolism.

Grover Cleveland 'Cleve' Backster Jr (1924-2013) was a specialist in hypno- and narco-interrogation for the US Central Intelligence Agency. In the early hours of 2 February 1966 he decided to hook up a *Dracaena fragrans* houseplant to a lie-detector machine, which led to him forming the theory that plants could pick up human thought. He published a book and was a hit on the talk-show circuit.

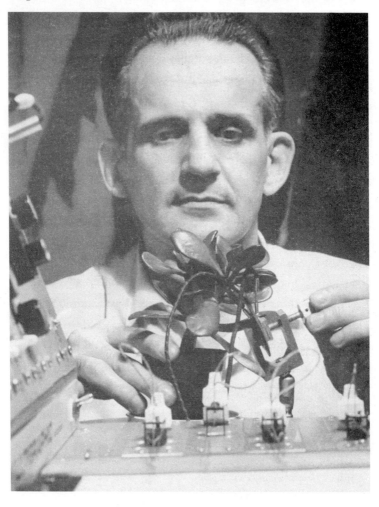

The American surgeon Nicholas Senn (1844-1908) pumped nearly 6 litres of hydrogen up his own anus using a balloon and a rubber tube, which an assistant helped keep sealed by pressing the tube against the anus. His plan was to develop a technique in which one would be able to ascertain if the bullets of gunshot wounds had also ruptured the intestines. He had previously tested this theory on dogs and proved that gas escaping from the intestine was hydrogen, by setting light to it. Senn also tested whether cancer was contagious by transplanting under his skin a cancerous lymph node from a patient. After two weeks of no ill effects, he concluded it could not be spread to another person.[20]

In 1936 Dr Edwin Katskee (1903-1936) decided to document the results of cocaine use and took an enormous amount. His plan was to write notes on his office wall as the drugs took effect, but his writing became increasingly illegible as the experiment went on and were found to be 'of no value'. He wrote that his eyes were growing dimmer, his heart weaker and that he had the idea that carbohydrates might be a cure for poison. Then he found the pencil too heavy to hold. He was found dead of a massive overdose the next morning.

---

20. In *Gut Reactions: Understanding symptoms of the digestive tract* (1990), W. G. Thompson writes that, as part of their pre-race preparation at the 1976 Olympics, East German swimmers had 1.8 litres of air pumped up their colons via their anus to make them more buoyant. 'It apparently helped crawl and backstroke specialists, but a breaststroker complained that his gas-filled gut caused his feet to stick out of the water. Perhaps sports authorities will need to test athletes for flatus, as well as steroids.'*

*Incidentally, all of this isn't even the most impressive use of a repurposed backside. This recognition should perhaps go to a 34-year-old gentleman named Jose Luis Astoreka, who in 1990 won an annual nut-cracking competition in Kortezubi, Spain, by crushing thirty walnuts in fifty-seven seconds between his buttocks. His success was attributed to a 'peculiar physical characteristic' of the Astoreka family.

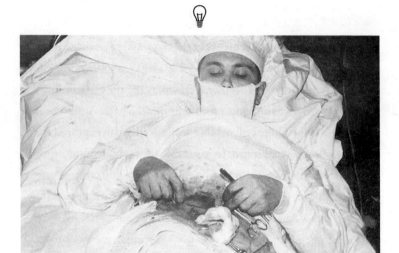

Dr Leonid Rogozov (1934-2000) was forced to remove his own appendix in 1961, while overwintering in Antarctica. Ever since then, doctors wintering at Antarctic stations have had to have their appendices removed before arrival, as they are usually the only doctor on station during winter. Evacuation to Australia is impossible for at least part of the year.

In 1736 the French scientist René Antoine Ferchault de Réaumur (1683-1757) dressed male frogs in tiny trousers made of pig's bladder and taffeta to collect the fluids secreted by the animals when dousing the female's eggs. The idea was to find out exactly what role sperm played in the reproduction process. This was repeated in 1760 by the Italian scientist Lazzaro Spallanzani (1729-1799), who not only put taffeta trousers on frogs but also on other amphibians, eventually working his way up to dogs. Despite these studies Spallanzani remained resolute in his 'ovist' belief, that sperm was merely a parasite and that everything needed to create life was in the egg.

The many notable achievements of the Egyptian surgeon, researcher and sexologist Ahmed Shafik (1933-2007), like performing the first bladder transplant in 1967, were eclipsed by the notoriety that came from his 1993 year-long study into how putting polyester, cotton or wool trousers on seventy-five rats affected their sex life. After twelve months of close scrutiny Shafik concluded that polyester trousers have the greatest effect in reducing rats' sexual activity.

A diagram from Ahmed Shafik's study on how different types of trousers on rats impinge on their sexual proclivities.

In 2019 mechanical engineers at Vanderbilt University, Nashville, Tennessee, performed an experiment in which they deliberately tripped volunteers running on treadmills by randomly throwing heavy blocks at their feet and studied their injuries. They concluded that people with prosthetic limbs fell more often and took longer to recover from stumbling.

Researchers at Rice University, Houston, Texas, discovered in 2022 that the dead bodies of wolf spiders can be repurposed as robotic gripping tools. Spiders don't have 'antagonistic' muscles, only flexor muscles that allow their legs to curl in, so if you seal a wolf spider with super glue and then deliver an internal puff of air, their legs will straighten like fingers before tightly curling again. The necrobiotic spider grippers can lift about 130 per cent of their body weight, while smaller spiders can handle even more.

Scientists have made human heart tissue from spinach, joint cartilage from spider silk, and artificial capillary systems using a candy-floss machine – it turns out the strands of candy floss are similar in size to human blood vessels.

After hearing the dismissive phrase 'that's like comparing apples and oranges' so often in public debate, Scott Sandford, a scientist at NASA's Ames Research Center at Moffett Field in California, decided to make the comparison with his spectrometer. His published findings *Apples and Oranges: A comparison* in 1995 contrasts the 2-7μm infrared transmission spectra of a Granny Smith apple and a Sunkist Navel orange, with the conclusion that 'Not only was this comparison easy to make, but it is apparent from the figure that apples and oranges are very similar.' Suggestions for more scientifically accurate phrases include 'Let's not compare walnuts with elephants' and 'Let's not compare tumour necrosis factor with linguini.'

SOME RESEARCH PAPERS PUBLISHED BY PUN-LOVING SCIENTISTS

Fantastic Yeasts and Where to Find Them:
The hidden diversity of dimorphic fungal pathogens
Current Opinion in Microbiology, December 2019

Getting to the Bottom of Anal Evolution
Zoologischer Anzeiger – A Journal of Comparative Zoology,
February 2015

An-arrgh-chy: The law and economics of pirate organisation
Journal of Political Economy, December 2007

miR miR on the Wall, Who's the Most Malignant
Medulloblastoma miR of Them All?
Neuro-Oncology, February 2018

The Mouth, the Anus, and the Blastopore: Open questions
about questionable openings
Animal Evolution Genomes, Fossils and Trees, August 2009

Taxa Biotechnologies is a US company that specialises in using synthetic biology to create plants that glow in the dark, with one stated goal being to replace streetlights with luminous trees. The first glow-in-the-dark plant was engineered in the 1980s, when a tobacco plant was created with a firefly gene.

The physics of Godzilla (who was awarded full Japanese citizenship in 2015) have been the subject of scientific quibbling for years as an interesting way of discussing the laws of scale. Ignoring the original actor-worn Godzilla costume, which incidentally was made of concrete, in recent films Godzilla is about 105m long, which means the monster weighs *c.*20,000 tonnes, or about 100 blue whales. To sustain this mass, Godzilla would need to eat around 25 tonnes of food for 20 million calories a day – the same requirements as a town of 10,000 people. Its heart would be 15m wide and weigh *c.*100 tonnes but would beat about twice a minute. Its aorta would be large enough for you to walk through, at *c.*3m across. Godzilla would shower the ground with 20,000 litres of urine daily and produce about 3 tonnes of faeces. All of which is moot, as, in the words of astrophysicist Neil deGrasse Tyson, 'Godzilla would collapse under his own weight into a puddle of guts.'

In a 2011 paper titled *Trajectory of a Falling Batman* student physicists at the University of Leicester concluded that Batman could fly, but at such velocity that he'd die a mangled mess on landing. If gliding with his rigid cape from a building 150m high, he could reach a distance of around 350m but would hit the ground at around 80km/hr. 'Clearly, gliding using a bat-cape is not a safe way to travel,' they concluded.

The authors of the 2018 paper *Ant-Man and the Wasp: Microscale respiration and micro fluidic technology* showed that, if we were able to shrink ourselves down to microscopic scale, our lungs would stop functioning and we'd probably suffocate to death from serious oxygen deprivation, akin to being in Everest's death zone.

The first to test the ejector seat of a US Air Force jet was a two-year-old black bear named Yogi, who was launched from a USAF B-58 at 10,600m going supersonic at 1400km/h, on 21 March 1962. Yogi survived the ejection, touching down dazed but unharmed seven minutes, forty-nine seconds later.

Canaries were used in mines from the late 1800s to detect gases and act as early warning detectors, but where did the idea come from? When the physician John Scott Haldane (1860-1936) was asked to help determine the cause of an explosion at Tylorstown Colliery in 1896, as part of his investigation he discovered that canaries are more sensitive and react faster than humans to dangerous buildups of gases like carbon monoxide. The idea for a canary in a cage was invented, but contrary to the popular image miners were fond of the birds and wanted to protect them. And so cages like the one shown here by Siebe Gorman & Co. Ltd of London were developed, where the bird's enclosure is supplied with an oxygen cylinder to revive it from noxious gases.

A canary air tester with oxygen tank for revival.

The elephant that never was. This is a 1758 design by an engineer from Béziers named Charles-François Ribart for a proposed Parisian structure to celebrate a victorious Louis XV after the War of the Austrian Succession had ended in 1748. Louis XV stands atop a colossal elephant, inside which are various decorated rooms. The painted forest at the rear is a dining room, complete with stream and mechanisms for playing birdsong. The table drops down into the room below to allow servants to change courses without intruding on the privacy of guests. Ribart proposed building the monument where the Arc de Triomphe now stands, and having a fountain pour from the elephant's trunk.

Pliny the Elder describes the bonnacon or bonasus, a bull-like creature that lived in the ancient kingdom of Paeonia (modern-day Macedonia). As its horns curled inward the animal instead relied on its bottom for defence, spraying boiling-hot dung that set fire to anything and anyone it touched. It's also from Pliny that we learn of a battle between an elephant and a dragon, the blood of which combined to create the red mineral and pigment cinnabar. He also provides us with the expression 'lick into shape', from his claim that bear cubs are born as shapeless lumps of white flesh, which their mothers must lick until they take cub form.

A bonnacon in the Northumberland Bestiary, *made in England c.1250-60.*

The now-extinct Moscow Water Dog was a Russian experimental breed created by the state-operated Red Star Kennels in Krasnaya Zvezda, Belarus, by interbreeding Newfoundland males with East European Shepherd and Caucasian Ovcharka females, and by mating the offspring with each other. The idea was to develop a water rescue/lifesaving dog, but according to Moscow University researcher Olga O. Krasnovskaya: 'That was not a good idea, as they were not willing to save drowning people, and mostly were looking to bite them, so this breed was never developed.'

In one sense, the oldest artworks in the world are the icons of Eastern Orthodox Christianity. Artists painting the holy scenes and portraits of saints on the wooden panels would rarely presume to sign the work with their own name but *would* keep to the tradition of adding the date of their painting as the point of Creation, which in Eastern Orthodoxy was believed to have taken place on 1 September in the year 5508 BC.

In Michelangelo's (1475-1564) sculpture *Moses* (shown opposite), and in iconographic tradition, the biblical figure Moses is sometimes depicted with horns. This stems from a mistranslation by St Jerome (*c.*347-419/420) when writing the Vulgate Bible from earlier Hebrew manuscripts, in which the word for 'shining' or 'emitting rays' was confused with 'horned'.

In Eastern Orthodox tradition, icons were commonly painted with St Christopher shown as a soldier in armour, with the head of dog (shown opposite). One suggestion as to the origin of the 'St Christopher dog-head' tradition is that it comes from, or was at least contributed to, by a misreading of the Latin term Cananeus ('Canaanite') as caninus ('canine'). One biography of St Christopher reports the tale of a man named Reprebus ('the scoundrel') in the reign of the Emperor Diocletian, who was taken prisoner by Roman soldiers battling tribes to the west of Egypt in Cyrenaica. Reprebus, who is described as being of enormous size with the head of a dog, was press-ganged into joining the Roman *numerus Marmaritarum* ('Unit of the Marmaritae'), a platoon of werewolf-like soldiers. When he and his unit were transferred to Syrian Antioch, Bishop Peter of Attalia baptised him Christopher. He was martyred there in 308.

The *Mona Lisa* is the only painting of the more than one million artworks in the collection of the Louvre to have ever been given its own postbox to cope with the amount of love letters from admirers. A 29-year-old Picasso was a suspect in the 1911 theft of the *Mona Lisa* from the Louvre, as four years earlier he had innocently (he claimed) purchased two statues that had also been stolen from the Louvre. However, in December 1913 the painting was discovered in the closet of Vincenzo Peruggia, an ex-Louvre employee who had simply walked out with it hidden under his white worker's smock.

The Virgin of Guadalupe, 1745. In the European popular image, the Virgin Mary has been depicted with white skin, but throughout the rest of the world icons and other paintings and statues of the Virgin Mary commonly depict her with dark skin. These paintings are known as Black Madonnas.

The *Mona Vanna* (*c.*1514-1515) is a nude version of *Mona Lisa*, credited to an apprentice of Da Vinci known as Salai. A preparatory sketch of the nude held by the Louvre is considered to have been drawn in part by Da Vinci's own hand, suggesting that Salai's painting is based on a lost original nude by Da Vinci himself.

An extraordinary painting only recently discovered, *Allegorical Painting of Two Ladies Wearing Beauty Patches* by an unknown English artist, dates to the 1650s and shows two women, one black and one white, both luxuriously dressed with finely coiffed hair and elegant jewellery. The work is highly unusual for the period in that it shows the two women as being of equal status; and for the curious details that decorate their faces. The half-moons, sickle, stars and other shapes are cosmetic beauty spots (patches to hide blemishes and pockmarks left by disease), which are condemned as a sin of pride in an inscription accompanying the image.

Yasuke, a man of African origin who served as a weapon-bearer to the Japanese *daimyō* Oda Nobunaga (1534-1582), was also said to be the first black samurai. Yasuke arrived in Japan in 1579, in the service of the Italian Jesuit missionary Alessandro Valignano (1539-1606), Visitor of Missions in the Indies, in India, and was one of several African slaves brought by the Portuguese to Japan. Thought to have originated from Mozambique, Yasuke learned to speak Japanese and was given his own residence. When Nobunaga was attacked by the forces of the samurai Akechi Mitsuhide (1528-1582), Yasuke fought beside him, and when Nobunaga was forced to commit suicide the black samurai joined the army of his successor to continue the fight against Akechi. He was captured and presented to the warlord, who ordered that he be spared execution and presented to the Christian church in Kyoto. This was the last record of Yasuke; his fate is unknown.

☧✡

The grave of Jesus Christ can be found in Japan. In 1934, a Shinto priest in Japan's Ibaraki Prefecture discovered written documents purporting to be the last will and testament of Jesus Christ, identifying the village of Shingō in Aomori Prefecture as his last resting place.

Jesus, it turns out, did not die on the cross; that was his previously unreported brother Isukiri, who had secretly taken his place. As Isukiri suffered the crucifixion, Jesus secretly fled for Japan, where he made a fake identity for himself and enjoyed a quiet life, marrying a farmer's daughter named Miyuk and raising three children, and farming garlic. Described as bald with features of a 'long-nosed goblin', Jesus Christ died in Japan at the age of 106.

You can visit his grave to this day. Daitenku Taro Jurai, as Jesus is known in Shingō, was buried in a mound of earth marked with a large wooden cross and bordered with a white picket fence. Every year around 20,000 pilgrims make the seven-hour train journey northwards from Tokyo to visit the grave, which is maintained by the local yogurt factory. The villagers of Shingō are certain of their godly heritage. 'I'm not really planning anything at all for the 25th [of December], as it doesn't really matter to us,' a 52-year-old villager named Junichiro Sawaguchi told a reporter in 2008. 'I know I am descended from Jesus, but as a Buddhist it's just not all that important.'

'Christ's Grave' in Shingō, Japan.

The American Spiritual clergyman John Murray Spear (1804-1887) attempted to build an electrically powered robot Messiah called the 'New Motive Power' that he claimed would herald a new Utopia. In his book *Messages from the Superior State; Communicated by John Murray, Through John M. Spear* (1853), Spear relates the instructions for humanity and other messages he received from a coterie of spirits he called 'The Association of Electrizers', a group that included the ghosts of Benjamin Franklin, Thomas Jefferson, John Quincy Adams, Benjamin Rush and Spear's namesake, the minister John Murray.

The year the book was published, Spear and a troupe of devoted followers withdrew to a secluded wooden lodge atop High Rock Hill in Lynn, Massachusetts, and began building the mechanical Messiah from copper, zinc, magnets and a dining-room table. After nine months of work, Spear ordered a female follower, whom he hailed the 'New Mary', to give birth to the machine in an elaborate ritual. The electric Messiah failed to rise. Spear then claimed to have received a message from the Association of Electrizers instructing him to immediately retire, and he disappeared.

At the Longquan Buddhist temple in China you can find a robotic monk called Xian'er, whose full title is Worthy Stupid Robot Monk, tasked with chatting to tourists and offering advice.

This is Daniel the Steam Man, or Rickshaw Man, Newark, USA, *c.*1868. Invented by Zadoc Dedrick, the early android was powered by a boiler system and designed to pull a cart in place of a horse. He was given clothes in order to appear less frightening; although when his fuel ran low passers-by would be met with the disconcerting sight of the operator unbuttoning Daniel's vest and shovelling coal into his chest.

Robots were exhibited for public entertainment as early as the eighteenth century. The most famous in London was Mr Haddock's Exhibition of Androides of the 1790s, which featured the Writing and Drawing Automaton, 'a mechanical boy about the size of a five-year-old who would draw pictures of a lion, tiger, elephant, camel, bear, horse or stag, and write any word, words or figures in a round legible hand'. The Highland Oracle was 'an automaton mind-reader in Scottish Highland dress who would strike his shield with his sword to calculate time or various arithmetical problems', while the Liquor Merchant 'would stand by a cask and deliver any of sixteen requested beverages'.

Men and women walking upside down across theatre ceilings were a popular Victorian entertainment. The 'air-walkers', or 'human flies', used specially made hooked boots that connected with fixtures hidden in the ceiling.

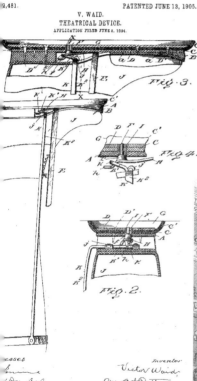

Left: A patent filing for a booted device that allows a performer to walk upside down across a theatre ceiling.

Below: A depiction of the 'air-walker' Mr Richard Sands treading the ceiling boards upside down at London's Drury Lane Theatre in 1853.

Pierre Testu Brissy (1770-1829) was a French balloonist who made the first night ascent to a backdrop of fireworks on 18 June 1786, during which he also made the first recorded electrical observations

when he flew into an electrical storm and noticed the iron rods of his craft drew crackling discharges from the atmosphere.[21] Where he really earns a place in this book is with his invention of 'horse-ballooning' twelve years later, which replaced the hot-air-balloon basket with a floating platform on which he rode his horse. Testu Brissy made fifty horseback balloon ascents in his career.

The ballooning couple Jean Eugène and Louise Poitévin revived horse-ballooning decades after Testu Brissy. Madame Poitévin even rode a bull attached to a hot-air balloon, while dressed symbolically as Europe. They took their show to England where they were immediately taken to court by the Society for the Prevention of Cruelty to Animals, and their act was banned.

21. Incidentally, on the subject of ballooning, in Jules Verne's novel *Around the World in Eighty Days* Phileas Fogg travels entirely by rail and steamer – a hot-air balloon is never actually used. It was added in film adaptations. And while we're on this, the title of another acclaimed work of Verne, *20,000 Leagues Under the Sea*, refers to the distance travelled while underwater, not the depth reached.

Diving horses from heights of 18m into water was an entertainment devised by William 'Doc' Carver (1851-1927) in 1881, and performed at American lakes and piers before becoming a permanent fixture at Atlantic City's Steel Pier. The greatest horse diver was Sonora Webster, who had responded to Carver's advertisement for an 'attractive young woman who can swim and dive. Likes horses, desires to travel'. In 1931, while diving with her horse Red Lips, she was permanently blinded when her head impacted the water and her retinas detached. She continued to dive with horses completely blind for another eleven years.

Sonora Webster and her diving horse.

Birdie Draper (1916-2005) was an American parachutist and stunt performer known for her signature act of driving a car at full speed into a brick wall primed with explosives. 'The girl was unconscious when the dust and flying bricks had settled,' relayed the *Independent Record* on 7 August 1938, 'and permitted rescuers to reach her, but was revived after she was taken to a first-aid room.' Draper was paired up with Captain Frank. F. Frakes, a professional plane-crasher who flew planes into empty buildings, sometimes with well-timed dynamite detonations for greater effect. The 'Death Fighters' duo toured together with a combined act. Frakes crashed sixty-five planes in shows (and destroyed many more in rehearsal) in a career that had started in the Great Depression. 'At the time it seemed the best way to make a living,' he told reporters.

The first human cannonball was a fourteen-year-old German girl named Rossa Richter (1862-1922), who was catapulted through the air in London's Royal Aquarium in 1877 in an act devised by the showman William Leonard Hunt (1838-1029).[22] Honourable mention should go to a similar stunt performed at around the same time in Paris by a performer named Mayol, who was catapulted from a 'mortar' up to a trapeze, but he missed his mark and flew straight into the balcony audience, and the act was abandoned.[23]

Joseph Pujol (1857-1945), better known as 'Le Pétomane' (literally 'The Fartomaniac') was a French flatulist who farted professionally on stage. He was renowned for his skilful control of his abdominal muscles, which enabled him to fart at will. It was not an abundance of intestinal gas that gave him this power, as one might be expect, but rather his ability to 'inhale' air through his rectum and then control the release of that air with his anal sphincter muscles.

---

22. The most interesting story of Hunt's later years is his claim to have discovered a lost city in Africa's Kalahari Desert while searching for diamonds and hunting ostriches in the region in 1855 with his adopted son turned companion Lulu, a female impersonator. He describes coming across 'A half-buried ruin – a huge wreck of stones, on a lone and desolate spot; a temple – or a tomb for human bones left by men to decay and rot.' He published his findings and presented them to a sceptical Royal Geographical Society. His story of The Lost City of the Kalahari has prompted search expeditions to this day (most recently by microlite), which so far have all returned disappointed.

23. This seems as good a place as any to mention that the magician who invented the act of sawing a woman in half, P. T. Selbit (real name Percy Tibbles) first pursued fame with his less successful act The Mighty Cheese, in which he invited audience members onstage to try to push over a giant wheel of cheese. This they were unable to do because Tibbles had hidden a large gyroscope inside it.

In 2015 a freight plane of Singapore Airlines was forced
to make an emergency landing when the smoke alarm was
set off by farting sheep.

In 1889 Alexander Graham Bell (1847-1922) tried to create sheep
with twice the normal number of nipples. He had noticed that twins
were more likely to be born to ewes with more than two nipples,
and so set about trying to crossbreed excessively nippled specimens
to create animals with higher yield. However, by 1904 he was yet to
have any success and was forced to concede that there was actually
no link between twinning and multinippled sheep.

A New Voyage and Description of the Isthmus of America (1699) is
the journal of the British voyager, surgeon and pirate Lionel Wafer
(1640-1705), who mentions the few days that he and the pirate
crew of the *Roebuck* fell in with the natives of the island of Mocha in
December 1686. There, to cure boredom, they rode sheep:

> But that which is most worthy of Note, is a Sort of Sheep they
> have, which the Inhabitants call *Cornera de Terra*. This Creature is
> about 4 Foot and an half high at the Back, and a stately Beast.
> These Sheep are so tame, that we frequently used to bridle one of
> them, upon whose Back two of the lustiest Men would ride at once
> round the island, to drive the rest to the Fold. His ordinary Pace is
> either an Amble or a good Hand-gallop; nor does he care for
> going any other Pace, during the Time his Rider is upon his Back.

The 'sheep' to which Wafer refers are almost certainly llamas, which
only makes the image stranger.

According to Captain Charles Johnson's *A General History of the Robberies and Murders of the Most Notorious Pyrates* (1724), Edward Teach (*c.*1680-1718), the English pirate known as Blackbeard, was fond of 'mischievous frolics' like shooting two of his crew for no apparent reason while the three drank together in his cabin. 'Damn you all!' explained Blackbeard. 'Unless I now and then kill one of my men, they will forget who I am.'

When the British explorer Sir John Franklin (1786-1847) vanished in the Arctic, some bizarre rescue attempts were made. This broadside from 1852 (of which this is the only known copy) celebrates the use of hydrogen balloons by Horatio Austin's search party to scatter message leaflets across the Arctic informing the survivors of the locations of relief vessels and food caches.

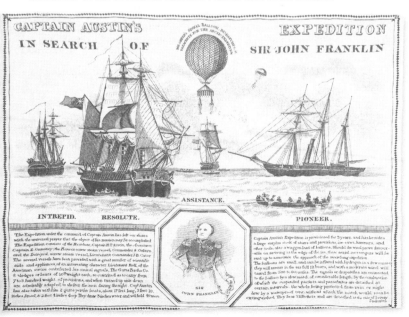

Over 1000 citations in the *Oxford English Dictionary* are attributed to William Dampier (1651-1715), the explorer-naturalist-pirate described by Samuel Taylor Coleridge as 'a man of exquisite mind'. Dampier was the first person to circumnavigate the globe three times, and the first Englishman to step foot on and explore parts of Australia; and for making notes on its flora, fauna and indigenous people, he is considered its first natural historian. Words that he introduced to the English language from his travels include avocado, barbecue, breadfruit, caress, cashew, catamaran, chopsticks, posse, settlement, snapper, soy sauce, stilts, subsistence, subspecies, swampy, thundercloud, snug and tortilla.

SOME USEFUL WORDS FOR VERY SPECIFIC INSTANCES

ABIBLIOPHOBIA (*English*) – The fear of running out of books to read

ACERSECOMIC (*English*) – A person who has never had a haircut

ACHAPLINARSE (*Chilean*) – To move around in the style of Charlie Chaplin

ARIGATA-MEIWAKU (*Japanese*) – The feeling you have when someone does you a favour you didn't ask them to do, which then causes you further problems, but you have to pretend to be grateful anyway

BADRUKA (*Swedish*) – The act of very slowly and reluctantly easing oneself into a body of cold water

DIE WALDEINSAMKEIT (*German*) – The feeling of being alone in the woods

ELEPHANTOCETOMACHIA (*English*) – A battle fought between an elephant and a whale

GLUGGAVEÐUR (*Icelandic*) – Literally 'window weather', which is better enjoyed from inside than out, like a blizzard

KOMOREBI (*Japanese*) – Sunbeams that filter through the trees

KOROBIKOBOU (*Japanese*) – Police slang for deliberately bumping into a suspect as an excuse to then arrest them for obstruction

KUMMERSPECK (*German*) – Literally 'grief bacon'. The extra weight one gains from eating excessively when sad.

MENCOLEK (*Indonesian*) – The name given to the prank of reaching around to tap someone on one shoulder while standing on their opposite side

SHEMOMEDJAMO (*Georgian*) – An exclamation for regretful gluttons; it essentially means, 'I accidentally ate the whole thing'

VAÐLAHEIÐARVEGAVINNUVERKFÆRAGEYMSLUSKÚRSLY KLAKIPPUHRINGURINN (*Icelandic*) – The keyring to the tool work shed in the road works of Vaðlaheiði, a mountain road in North Iceland

ZENZIZENZIZENZIC – An obsolete form of mathematical notation, representing the eighth power of a number (i.e. x^8 is the zenzizenzizenzic of x). This dates from the time when powers were written out as words, not superscript numbers. The word was first proposed by a sixteenth-century Welsh mathematician named Robert Recorde, in his 1557 book *The Whetstone of Witte*, in which he says his invented word 'doeth represent the square of squares squaredly'.

*'I speak Spanish to God, Italian to women,
French to men, and German to my horse.'*

Charles V (1500-1558), Holy Roman Emperor

Reinhold Aman (1936-2019), a professor of German and publisher of a scholarly journal dedicated to the study of offensive language called *Maledicta*, declared Hungarians as having the foulest phrases of all cultures. Some examples:

- When your employer hands you an unreasonable amount of work, you say: ***Bekergettek tátott szájjal a faszerdőbe***. It means: 'They chased me into the dick-forest with a wide-open mouth.'

- When you encounter an idiot: ***Agyilag zokni***. 'Intellectually, you're a sock.'

- When you successfully convince someone to perform a difficult task on your behalf: ***Más faszával verni a csalánt***, which means 'beating the nettles with someone else's dick'.

- When you wish to thoughtfully compliment someone on their singing voice: ***Erotikus a hangod, bassza a fülem***. 'Your voice is erotic, it has sex with my ears.'

- When greeting a group of people, say ***Összefújta a szemetet a szél***. 'I see the wind has blown the trash together.'

- An old Hungarian equivalent of 'give them an inch and they'll take a mile' is ***fogadd be a tótot, kitúr a házadból***. 'Let in the Slovak and he'll chase you out of your house.'

- When wishing to simply insult someone: ***Szopna le a vacogós cápa***. 'May a shark blow you with chattering teeth.'

Hungarian children are warned to behave, or they'll be visited by their version of the bogeyman, *Rézfaszú bagoly*, a giant owl with a copper penis. They're also told that eating carrots will make them better at whistling.

According to a 2019 survey of UK adults:

44%

have kept their childhood Teddy bears (either at their own house or their parents' home).

34%

still sleep with a soft toy every night.

24%

who had lost their toy said they felt 'devastated'.

17%

admit they still cuddle a teddy when they're upset.

15%

say they can't sleep without theirs.

11%

have taken their soft toy on holiday.

5%

have smuggled it into work.

'Sleep you black-eyed pig,
Fall into a deep pit full of ghosts.'
Icelandic lullaby translated by W. H. Auden
in *Letters from Iceland*, 1937.

The longest Icelandic word, Auden also reports in the same book,
was *Haestarjettarmalaflutunesmanskifstofustulkonutidyralykill* –
'A latch-key belonging to a girl working in the office of a barrister.'

The Spanish word for wife is *esposa*.
The Spanish word for handcuffs is *esposas*.

There is no word in French for 'shrug'.

There is no Polish or Russian word for 'toe';
they use 'finger on the leg'.

In 1869 there was no official term for the velocipede enthusiast
at the time; the sport was new, and 'cyclist' was not to arrive
for some years. In one of the earliest books on bicycling, the
tremendously titled *The Velocipede … How to Ride a Velocipede
– Straddle a Saddle, then Paddle and Skedaddle* (1869), the
English barrister Joseph Firth Bottomley disregarded the more
obvious choice of 'velocipedist' in favour of the term 'which we
are assured has become quite common across the Atlantic, viz.,
"VELOCIPEDESTRIANISTICALISTINARIANOLOGIST".'

The English word 'escape' comes from 'ex cape', as in to slip out of one's cape and flee an attacker. The word comes via Old French *eschaper*, back to the Vulgar Latin *excappare*, literally 'get out of one's cape, leave a pursuer with just one's cape', from Latin *ex-* 'out of' + Late Latin *cappa* 'mantle'.

In 1803 a German convict sent to Australia named Joseph Samuel was sentenced to hang for murder. The first execution attempt failed when the hemp rope snapped and Joseph fell, injuring his ankle. A second rope loosened, and Samuel's feet touched the ground. A third rope was fetched, but this broke too. Everyone agreed that this was a clear sign that God wished mercy on Samuel, so the governor generously reduced his sentence to life imprisonment.

A lifesaving book. This copy of the 1913 French pocket edition of Rudyard Kipling's *Kim* was carried by the legionnaire Maurice Hamonneau in his breast pocket during an attack near Verdun during the First World War. When he regained consciousness he found that the book had stopped a bullet, saving his life by only twenty pages.

✦

THE MURDEROUS ORIGINS OF THE OXFORD ENGLISH DICTIONARY

In March 1879 the schoolteacher James Murray (1837-1915) agreed to head the project to compile a new definitive lexicon of the English language: the *Oxford English Dictionary*. He quickly realised it would take him years to collect just a fraction of the necessary entries, and so decided to crowd-source. Via bookshops and libraries in both Britain and North America, Murray put out an invitation to the public to submit words with their definitions and example quotations. By 1880 he had received 2.5 million quotation slips, and they kept coming.

One of the most prolific contributors, providing many thousands of quotations, was a man Murray had never heard of before. Dr William Chester Minor, of the Broadmoor Asylum for the Criminally Insane, devoted all his time to the dictionary project, scouring his large personal library for the requested quotations. Over years of correspondence, Murray and Minor became friends, but whenever Murray suggested meeting the doctor declined. Finally, after over a decade, Minor relented, and in January 1891 Murray took a train to Crowthorne in the county of Berkshire. Only on his arrival did he discover, to his astonishment, that Dr Minor was not an employee of Broadmoor Asylum – he was an inmate.

Minor had been a surgeon in the American Civil War and was later institutionalised in a lunatic asylum for eighteen months. Then, after moving to London for recuperation, one night in 1871 he shot and killed an innocent passerby named George Merrett, believing him to be a thief. Minor was confined to Broadmoor Asylum but was judged by staff not to be dangerous and lived in relatively comfortable quarters, using his US army pension to buy and read books. Remarkably, Merrett's widow occasionally visited Minor, bringing books for him each time. When Minor came across Murray's appeal for public contributions, he had nothing but time to immerse himself in the challenge. His work filled the dictionary. In 1899 Murray paid tribute to Minor's gigantic contribution, saying: 'We could easily illustrate the last four centuries from his quotations alone.'

SOME DIRTY SLANG OF GEORGIAN LONDON

Apple dumpling shop – *A woman's bosom*

Arsy varsey – *To fall arsy varsey, i.e. head over heels*

Beard splitter – *A man much given to wenching*

Blindman's holiday – *Night, darkness*

Blowsabella – *A woman whose hair is dishevelled and hanging about her face*

Cackling farts – *Eggs*

Casting up one's accounts – *Vomiting*

Cup of the creature – *A cup of good liquor*

Curtain lecture – *A woman who scolds her husband when in bed is said to read him a curtain lecture*

Duke of limbs – *A tall, awkward, ill-made fellow*

Dutch feast – *Where the entertainer gets drunk before his guests*

Frenchified – *Infected with the venereal disease*

Louseland – *Scotland*

Marriage musick – *The squalling and crying of children*

Milk the pidgeon – *To endeavour at impossibilities*

Puff guts – *A fat man*

Shag bag – *A poor sneaking fellow, a man of no spirit*

Slubber de gullion – *A dirty nasty fellow*

Tormentor of catgut – *A fiddle player*

The Mariko Aoki phenomenon is a Japanese term for the sudden urge to defecate that some report feeling upon entering bookshops.

There is an art to the great book title, as demonstrated by the late English humourist Alan Coren (1938-2007), who when choosing a name for his collection of essays in 1975 noticed that the most popular books in Britain at that time were about cats, golf and Nazis. So, he called his book *Golfing for Cats* and slapped a swastika on the cover. We also learn that care should be taken to avoid tempting an ironic fate when titling a book. Bill Hillman, the American author of the 2014 guide *Fiesta: How to survive the bulls of Pamplona*, was gored by the bulls of Pamplona that same year – and again the next year. And in the 2017 British national election, the Conservative politician Gavin Barwell, author of *How to Win a Marginal Seat* (2016), lost his marginal seat.

SOME STRANGE BOOK TITLES

Ecloga de Calvis; or, In Praise of Bald Men (c.910) by the French monk Hucbald

The Loathsomnesse of Long Haire ... with the Concurrent Judgement of Divines both Old and New Against It. With an Appendix Against Painting, Spots, Naked Breasts, etc. (1654) by Rev. Thomas Hall

Arse Musica; or, The Lady's Back Report ... (1722) by the Countess of Fizzle Rumpff (Jonathan Swift)

An Essay on the Art of Ingeniously Tormenting; with Proper Rules for the Exercise of that Pleasant Art (1753) by Jane Collier

Sun-beams May Be Extracted from Cucumbers, But the Process is Tedious (1799) by David Daggett

Memoirs of an Old Wig (1815) by Richard Fenton

Ducks; and How to Make Them Pay (1890) by William Cook

Ghosts I Have Met, and Some Others (1898) by John Kendrick Bangs

How to Cook Husbands (1898) by Elizabeth Strong Worthington

Fishes I Have Known (1905) by Arthur Henry Bevan

An Irishman's Difficulties with the Dutch Language (1908) by Cuey-Na-Gael

Pigs: How to make them pay (1918) published by C. Arthur Pearson Limited

Does the Earth Rotate? No! (1919) by William Westfield

What Would Christ Do About Syphilis? (*c.*1930) by Dr Ira D. Cardiff

Thought Transference (Or What?) in Birds (1931) by Edmund Selous

Your Answer to Invasion – Ju-Jitsu (1941) by James Hipkiss

Mrs Rasmussen's Book of One-Arm Cookery (1946) by Mary Lasswell

Harnessing the Earthworm (1947) by Thomas J. Barrett

The Jewish-Japanese Sex and Cook Book and How to Raise Wolves (1972) by Jack Douglas

Highlights in the History of Concrete (1979) by C. C. Stanley

How to Good-bye Depression: If you constrict anus 100 times everyday. malarkey? or effective way? (2000) by Hiroyuki Nishigaki

The Bible Cure for Irritable Bowel Syndrome (2002) by Don Colbert, MD

Does God Ever Speak Through Cats? (2006) by David Evans

Ghosts: Minnesota's other natural resource (2007) by Brian Leffler

After You Shoot: Your gun's hot. The perp's not. Now what? (2010) by Alan Korwin

Open Wide for the Handsome Sabertooth Dentist Who is also a Ghost (2017) by Chuck Tingle

The longest recorded personal name is that of German-born American Hubert Blaine Wolfeschlegelsteinhausenbergerdorff Sr (abbreviated) (1914-1997). His full name had twenty-six forenames, one for each of the letters of the alphabet, followed by a 666-letter surname.[24]

Bangkok hasn't been called Bangkok by the Thai people for hundreds of years. Its full name is Krungthepmahanakhon Amonrattanakosin Mahintharayutthaya Mahadilokphop Noppharatratchathaniburirom Udomratchaniwetmahasathan Amonphimanawatansathit Sakkathattiyawitsanukamprasit. It's referred to as Krung Thep Maha Nakhon, or Krung Thep.

Osama Vinladen López (b.2002) is a Peruvian footballer who is currently a midfielder for the Peruvian Primera División team Unión Comercio. Vinladen was named after Osama bin Laden (the pronunciation is the same in Spanish). He has a brother named Sadam Huseín, and a sister called Georgia Bush. He is yet to play against the Brazilian footballer Marx Lenin dos Santos Gonçalves.

---

24. Specifically: Adolph Blaine Charles David Earl Frederick Gerald Hubert Irvin John Kenneth Lloyd Martin Nero Oliver Paul Quincy Randolph Sherman Thomas Uncas Victor William Xerxes Yancy Zeus Wolfeschlegelsteinhausenbergerdorffwelchevoralternwarengewissenhaftschaferswessenschafewarenwohlgepflegeundsorgfaltigkeitbeschutzenvonangreifendurchihrraubgierigfeindewelchevoralternzwolftausendjahresvorandieerscheinenvanderersteerdemenschderraumschiffgebrauchlichtalsseinursprungvonkraftgestartseinlangefahrthinzwischensternartigraumaufdersuchenachdiesternwelchegehabtbewohnbarplanetenkreisedrehensichundwohinderneurassevonverstandigmenschlichkeitkonntefortpflanzenundsicherfreuenanlebenslanglichfreudeundruhemitnichteinfurchtvorangreifenvonandererintelligentgeschopfsvonhinzwischensternartigraum.

Nominative determinism is the idea that people are drawn towards occupations that are connected with their names. The term originated in 1994 when John Hoyland, the editor of *New Scientist*, noted that a new book, *Pole Positions: The polar regions and the future of the planet*, was written by one Daniel Snowman, and another book received two weeks earlier, *London Under London: A subterranean guide*, was authored by Richard Trench. Readers sent in other examples, like the zoological history *The Imperial Animal* by Lionel Tiger and Robin Fox. Another example would be the article on incontinence in the *British Journal of Urology* written by A. J. Splatt and D. Weedon.

Amy Freeze is an American television meteorologist, as is Larry Sprinkle.

Ann Webb founded the British Tarantula Society.

Leeds Cathedral's current organist is David Pipe.

Neuroscientist Sir Henry Head (1861-1940) treated soldiers with brain injuries during the First World War, and discovered areas of sensitive skin around the body that became known as Head Zones. He was appointed editor of the medical journal *Brain*, a role later taken by Russell Brain, 1st Baron Brain (1895-1966).

Headshot of Sir Henry Head, editor of Brain.

In 2015 a nineteen-year-old American man named Bud Weisser was arrested by St Louis police for trespassing at a Budweiser brewery.

American academic Dr Marijuana Pepsi Vandyck gained her PhD in 2019 with a dissertation on unusual names.[25]

Vania Stambolova is a Bulgarian hurdler. At the London 2012 Olympics, she tripped during the 400m hurdles event and failed to finish.

A former spokesman on knife crime for the UK Association of Chief Police Officers was Chief Constable Alfred Hitchcock (1958-2017). He went by 'Alf'.

New Scientist then coined the term 'nominative contradeterminism', for those whose career moves contradicted their name. Perhaps the best example of this is Jaime Lachica Sin (1928-2005), Archbishop of Manila, otherwise known as Cardinal Sin.

Byzantine Emperor from 741 to 775 Constantine V the Dung-Named, Anointed with Urine, was so nicknamed because as an infant he reportedly defecated in his baptismal font.[26]

---

25. On a nominally related note, a researcher at the British National Archives named George Redmonds discovered in a list of fourteenth-century names a girl named Diot Coke, born in 1379 in West Riding, Yorkshire. Diot is a diminutive of Dionisia, the origin of the modern name Denise.

26. An interesting thing about the two large copper bowls that form the baptismal font at Norwich Cathedral, UK, is that they were originally used for manufacturing toffee at the nearby Rowntree Mackintosh chocolate factory. When the factory shut down in 1994 the bowls were donated to the cathedral, and the holy fonduing of infants commenced.

The 'Kybiosaktes' part of the name of Seleucus VII Kybiosaktes (who is thought to have been King of Syria c.83-69BC) is a derogatory nickname meaning the foul-smelling work of cutting tuna fish. The notoriously unpleasant fellow was allegedly murdered because of his lack of manners by his bride, the Ptolemaic princess Berenice IV (75-55BC), who was the sister of the famous Cleopatra VII of Egypt.

Anglo-Saxon nicknames involving male genitalia are relentlessly common in contemporary texts. The survey of c.1110 in *Winton Domesday* lists a gentleman named Balloc ('Testicle') and another named Alfred Caddebelloc ('Testicle testicle'). More elaborate is Humphry Aurei Testiculi ('Goldenbollocks') and Æthelfrith Taddebelloc ('Toad-bollocks').

SOME VIKING NICKNAMES

From the Icelandic *Landnamabok* we learn of Herjólfr holkinrazi ('Man with a crouched arse') and Eysteinn meinfretr ('Harm-fart'). Others include:

Able to fill a bay with fish by magic	Seal's testicles
Able to remain warm in winter	Short penis
Big, ugly, clownish person	Squat-wiggle
Butter-penis	The man who mixes his drinks
Desirous of beer	The man without trousers
Lust-hostage	Whining turd

King Ragnar Lothbrok 'Shaggy-britches' was so named
for the hairy trousers made for him by his wife.

The ninth-century Viking ruler Ivar Ragnarsson was
known as Ivar the Boneless, but we're not sure why.

A hundred doesn't mean 100; the word 'hundred' derives
from the Old Norse word *hundrath*, which means
'long hundred', or specifically, 120.

The English word 'gun' comes from the female
Norse name Gunnhildr, meaning 'war, battle'.

Hortatory names are Puritan names formed of religious slogans.
Nicholas Barebone (*c*.1640-1698), for example, was an English
physician, economist and founder of fire insurance, who enjoyed the
full name of Nicholas If-Jesus-Christ-Had-Not-Died-For-Thee-Thou-
Hadst-Been-Damned Barebone, given to him by his father Praise-
God Barebone. The register of St Helen's, Bishopsgate, London, for
the year 1611 includes the names Be-courteous Cole, Safely-on-high
Snat, Fight-the-good-fight-of-faith White, Humiliation Scratcher
and Kill-sin Pemble. In New England, USA, lived Notwithstanding
Griswold, Maybe Barnes and Mene Mene Tekel Upharsin Pond.
There is also a nineteenth-century record of a New England sea
captain named Through-Much-Tribulation-We-Enter-Into-the-
Kingdom-of-Heaven Clapp. He was known as Tribby to his friends.

Eleanor Roosevelt's (1884-1962) maiden name was Roosevelt.
Her husband Franklin, the 32nd president of the USA,
was her fifth cousin once removed.

This enormous fish-shaped building is the Fish-Shaped Building, headquarters of India's National Fisheries Development Board, in the landlocked state of Telangana. Admirers hailed it as a unique example of mimetic architecture. Critics called it a 'a shark that swallowed a blimp'.

In 1996, in response to a fine of 5,000 kronor for not having registered a name for their five-year-old child, a Swedish couple submitted the name 'Brfxxccxxmnpcccclllmmnprxvclmnckssqlbb11116', pronounced 'Albin'. This was rejected by the court, as was the next suggestion of 'A' (also pronounced Albin). They eventually settled for Albin Gustaf Tarzan Hallin.

Hugh Jackman has said he refers to his penis as 'Old James Roger'. Channing Tatum calls his 'Gilbert'. Tom Jones christened his 'Wendell'. A 2015 survey by the retailer Jacamo found that the most popular nickname that men gave their appendage was 'Troy', followed by 'Hercules', then 'The Rock'. 'Russell the Muscle' came in fourth.

Twenty-three baby boys in the USA were recorded as being named Penis in 2010, a figure that shrank to seven by 2012.

According to Ancestry.co.uk, the family name Penis was most commonly found in the USA, the UK and Canada between 1840 and 1920. The largest number of Penis families were found in USA in 1880. In 1891 there was one Penis family living in London, which was '100 per cent of all the recorded Penises in the United Kingdom'.

The Chemehuevi, a Native American tribe along the Colorado River, were recorded as having two members in possession of traditional male names that translated into English as 'Rat Penis' and 'Fish Vagina'. Both originated in religious myths and were considered unremarkable.

In the late seventeenth century the theologian Thomas Burnet (1635-1715) deduced that, since there would obviously be political government in Heaven, it would have to be divided into nations. The English, French, Germans and Italians would therefore have to be kept separated 'in the air'.

St Martin of Tours (316/336-397), known as Martin the Merciful, was said to have once exorcised a man by shoving his arm down his throat and forcing the demon out through his anus.

☠

The notorious *Dictionnaire Infernal* of Jacques Collin de Plancy, first published in 1818, lists the hierarchy of demons. It is here, for example, that we learn of the political positions in Hell, with descriptions of demons like Adramelech, 'king of fire', eighth of the ten arch-demons, and grand chancellor of Hell.

Adramelech, grand chancellor of Hell, from the 1863 edition of the Dictionnaire Infernal.

☪

In Jewish and Christian mythology the Lords of Shouting, also known as the Masters of Howling, are a choir of 15,500,000 angels who congregate at dusk to sing.

☪

Christian scripture doesn't describe angels as having wings, and consequently the earliest Christian art of angels from the mid-third century show them wingless and indistinguishable from humans. Only in the late fourth century do artists start reimagining the creatures with birdlike wings. (The Cherubim and Seraphim are described as winged bestial creatures in the Bible, but they're not angels as they don't perform the angelic functions.)

THE MAYAN LORDS OF DEATH

One-Death and Seven-Death govern the underworld Xibalba ('place of fright')

Flying Scab and Blood Gatherer poison the blood of their victims with illness

Pus Master and Jaundice Master cause swelling of the body

Bone Sceptre and Skull Sceptre turn corpses into skeletons

Wing and Packstrap cause people who go for walks to fatally cough up blood

Sweepings Demon and Stabbing Demon hide in the dirty areas of homes and wait to stab to death those who are behind on their household chores

Roamed by demonic predators, the Mayan underworld Xibalba is a vast land from which there is no escape. The *Popol Vuh* ('Book of the People') reveals it to be a giant city of deception and trickery; just travelling to its outskirts involves overcoming a series of booby traps. First one has to cross a river of scorpions, then a thick river of blood, then an oozing river of pus. Farther on, the traveller must navigate a junction of four roads, which each speak aloud to lead one astray. Finally, the visitor reaches the council place of Xibalba, where protocol dictates he or she must greet the seated Lords. This, however, is a confusing and humiliating process, because the seats around the Lords have been filled with lifelike dummies, making it difficult to know who to approach. The deceased is then offered a bench to rest and recover from the embarrassment, but this is another prank – the seat turns out to be a scalding-hot cooking plate.

Both God and the Devil have been the subjects of real lawsuits in recent history. *United States ex rel. Gerald Mayo v. Satan and His Staff*, for example, was filed in 1971 by Gerald Mayo, an inmate at Western Penitentiary, Pittsburgh, who complained that Satan had 'deprived him of his constitutional rights' – it was dismissed after the court noted that as a foreign prince Satan could claim sovereign immunity. In 1970 Arizona lawyer Russel T. Tansie sued God for $100,000 for 'negligence' on behalf of his secretary, Betty Penrose, whose house had been damaged by lightning. When the defendant 'failed to turn up in court', Penrose won the case by default.

☪

The Devil's Advocate was originally a real position established in the Catholic Church in 1587. The *advocatus diaboli* was the Promoter of the Faith, a canon lawyer whose job it was to present arguments against the canonisation (sainthood) of candidates to find any flaws in the evidence submitted and offer scepticism as to the miracles supposedly performed. Today this role and that of the opposing representative known as 'God's advocate' (*advocatus Dei*; also known as the Promoter of the Cause) are both performed by the Promoter of Justice (*promotor iustitiae*) who assesses the saintliness of the candidate alone.

In 1998, in a letter published in the magazine *Physics Today*, two physicists at Spain's University of Santiago de Compostela calculated Heaven's temperature to be 504.5 kelvin (*c*.230°C). Jorge Mira Pérez and José Viña based their math calculations on Isaiah 30:26, which says that Heaven is illuminated by 'the light of the Sun [which] shall be sevenfold'. They applied Stefan's law, which states that the temperature of an object in thermal equilibrium is related to the fourth root of the amount of light it receives. 'A lot of colleagues have said they would prefer to stay on Earth,' said Pérez.

☪

St Augustine, one of the most important Fathers of the Latin Church, believed that in paradise our liver and other organs will become transparent as we completely reveal ourselves to God, which, he adds, makes not having to eat there all the more fortunate. There is no flatulence in Heaven either, he explains, because under the gaze of God even bowels are rendered perfect.

☦

In the Cathedral Basilica of the Assumption of Cusco, Peru, hangs a painting of *The Last Supper* created in 1753 with one detail that distinguishes it from all others of the same scene – Jesus and his disciples are dining on guinea pig. The roasted rodent lies paws-up on the platter at the centre of the table, just as the local delicacy continues to be found on many Peruvian restaurant tables today. The artist Marcos Zapata (*c.*1710-1773) was a Peruvian Quechua painter and member of the Cusco School, which combined European styles and traditions with native beliefs and customs as a way of syncretising the Inca way of life with Catholicism. Still, it's surprising that Zapata's guinea pig squeaked past the notice of Catholic authorities.

☦

'Playing chess with the Pope' is an Icelandic slang term for defecating.

☦

Pope John Paul II (1920-2005) and Pope Francis (b.1936) are members of the Harlem Globetrotters basketball team.

The Pope Lick Monster is a legendary man-goat-sheep hybrid said to live beneath a railway trestle bridge over Pope Lick Creek in Kentucky, USA. At least five people have died since 1988 after being hit by trains while trying to find the creature.

The British Library holds the only surviving copy of the first book on beards, *Apologia de Barbis* ('In Defence of Beards'), written *c.*1160 by Abbot Burchard of Bellevaux Abbey, France. The work is an attempt to quell a furious squabble between the Cistercian monks of the abbey, who were clean-shaven, and the lower-ranked lay brothers, who were bearded. The abbot had gently reprimanded some poorly behaved lay brothers in a letter, writing that the bearded men were metaphorically 'fuel for the fire', referencing a quote of the prophet Isaiah. The lay brothers took this to mean that the abbot was threatening to literally burn off their beards and revolted. The book is the abbot's soothing response, extolling the virtues of beards to a ridiculous extent. 'A beard is appropriate to a man as a sign of his comeliness,' he coos, 'as a sign of his strength, as a sign of his wisdom, as a sign of his maturity, and as a sign of his piety.' So, what did this mean for his monks, who shaved? The abbot had to think quickly. The answer was 'inner beards'. It was what grew on the inside, he said, that mattered more than the external appearance. Just as it was more important to *have* faith than to *act* as if one did, so it was better to have the virtues of the bearded than to have the beard itself.

The oldest known sentence in the first alphabet was deciphered only in 2021. The Canaanite inscription was found on a double-edged ivory comb made *c.*1700BC in Lachish, a city-state of Judah. It reads: 'May this tusk root out the lice of the hair and the beard.'

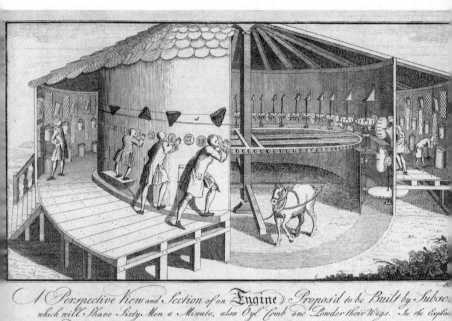

A proposed horse-powered shaving device to shave sixty men per minute, 1749.

Hans Steininger, a sixteenth-century burgomaster of Braunau am Inn, Austria, was said to have the world's longest beard, which he would roll up and tuck into his pocket when walking around. In 1567 a fire broke out in town, and in the confusion Hans tripped over his beard, fell down some stairs and broke his neck. You can visit his beard on display at the local district museum.

Hans Langseth (1846-1927), a Norwegian American farmer, became a freak-show feature with his record-setting 5.33m beard, *c.*1912 (see opposite). His beard was donated to the Smithsonian Institution.

According to a biography of Chairman Mao Zedong (1893-1976), his personal barber was called Big Beard Wang. At one point Big Beard Wang confessed to his employer that he was plotting to kill him, but when Mao learned that this confession had been forced out of him through sleep deprivation, he absolved him and said: 'Big Beard Wang has been cutting my hair and shaving me for years and has never so much as nicked my face. If he had wanted to kill me, he could have done it long before.'

Hairstyles of eighteenth-century Europe grew fantastically tall and elaborate under the influence of Marie Antoinette (1755-1793) and her trusted hairdresser Léonard Autié (1751-1820). Designs included 'Spaniel's Ears', 'Sportsman-in-the-Coppice', 'Mad Dog' and the 'Drowned Chicken'. A Madame de Lauzun of Paris was noted as an extreme example, with a pile of real and fake hair stacked atop her head decorated with model ducks at sea, hunting scenes, a mill with the miller's wife teasing a priest, and the miller leading his donkey. An essential accessory was the 'scratcher', a long stick with a hooked metal end to poke through the hair and bring relief to an itchy scalp.

One popular hairstyle in eighteenth-century Europe was inspired by the arrival in July 1741 of an Indian rhinoceros named Miss Clara, who sparked two decades of 'rhinomania' as she toured the cities and courts of the continent. Artists immortalised her likeness, poets devoted verses to her, and musicians wrote songs in her honour. Parisian women wore their hair *à la rhinocéros*, with hair and accessories forming a horn on their head.

An eighteenth-century satire of the trend for elaborate headdresses.

In Chinese slang, a comb-over is referred to as 'the localities supporting the central government'. In Japanese slang it's a 'barcode'. In Israel it's 'borrow and save'. In French you can call it 'bringing the suburbs to the town centre', while the Swedes call a comb-over the 'Robin Hood hairstyle', because it takes from the rich and gives to the poor.

The Great Parisian Moustache Strike took place on 17 April 1907. At 6.30 p.m., waiters across Paris immediately walked off the job and gathered on pavements until their employment demands were met, chief of which was the right to wear moustaches.

In the Albanian language there are at least eighteen categories for eyebrows. These include *vetull·përpjekur* 'having eyebrows that join together'; *vetull·kalem* 'having beautiful pencil-thin eyebrows'; and *vetull·hënë* 'having arched eyebrows like the crescent moon'.[27]

The Greek physician Galen (AD c.129-216) wrote of his belief that the skin's pores became blocked with sooty smoke particles generated by warm blood, until so much pressure built up that the soot erupted out of the skin in a solid string: this was how hair was made. The darker the hair, the higher the soot level, and therefore the hotter the temperature. Blond people therefore lacked natural warmth.

---

27. Incidentally, the Albanian word for a nanny is *dado*, while for 'dad' it's *babi*.*

    Babi also has a meaning in the Malay language, which the Albanian-British singer Dua Lipa discovered in 2018 after posting a loving tribute to her 'babi'. Her Malaysian fans demanded to know why she referred to her father as a 'pig'.

A US patent filed by Frank J. Smith and Donald J. Smith in 1977 for their invention of a comb-over technique folding three sections of hair.

U.S. Patent　　　　May 10, 1977　　　　4,022,227

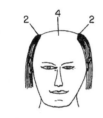

FIG. 1

FIG. 2

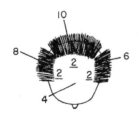

FIG. 3

FIG. 5

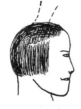

FIG. 4

FIG. 6

Italy rejoice: your countryman Daniele Tuveri holds the record
for longest nipple hair at 17cm, measured in Cagliari, Italy, on
13 March 2013.

Though negatively stigmatised as a sign of ageing, greying hair
indicates healthy active hair growth. Grey hair is thicker and grows
faster than pigmented hair. The mechanism for this is unknown.

The Brazilian wax was invented in the J Sisters salon in New York in
1990, with the first American client having to lie down on the office
desk with her leg up over a fax machine for the procedure. Strangely,
deliberate baldness had been brought to Brazil almost two hundred
years earlier, when the Portuguese royal court arrived in Brazil in
1808, with the European women all disembarking with their heads
shaved and wearing turbans, due to a lice outbreak during the
transatlantic voyage. The women of Rio de Janeiro assumed this was
the fashion and followed suit.

One of the strangest criminals in American history was the Phantom
Barber of Pascagoula, a mysterious figure who broke into homes
in Mississippi in 1942 and cut the hair of victims while they slept.
The Phantom never harmed anyone, only slicing open window
screens and making off with locks of hair, until an intruder attacked
a husband and wife with a metal pipe and the Phantom was blamed.
A man named William Dolan was arrested and charged but always
maintained his innocence, and when he passed a lie detector test he
was released. The Phantom Barber remains at large.

Humans are the only animals with chins and uvulas
(the fleshy 'teardrop' hanging at the back of your throat).

The British chemist Sir Humphry Davy (1778-1829), in whose memory
a lunar crater is named, dressed daily in an outfit of pure green: 'So as
to resemble vegetable life as closely as it was possible to do.' When on
countryside shoots he added a large crimson hat to the outfit, so as not
to be mistaken for scenery, although as one friend pointed out he was
at risk of being shot by an anti-cleric mistaking him for a cardinal.

Victorian thinker Herbert Spencer (1820-1903), who coined the
phrase 'survival of the fittest', had a pair of 'angry overalls' that he
wore whenever he was in a foul mood. Sir Harold Nicolson (1886-
1968) wrote of him sitting 'upstairs in his angry overalls, too angry
to come down to luncheon. And next morning he would dress in a
neat suit of grey tweed, and be again his bright and petulant self.'

John Quincy Adams (1767-1848) was the first
US president to wear trousers.

In 1931 New Zealand suffered an epidemic of exploding trousers.
Farmers witnessed their garments spontaneously erupting into
flames after working to clear their fields of the weed ragwort. The
culprit was found to be a commonly used weedkiller that contained
sodium chlorate, a volatile substance that can ignite from a naked
flame or even from being knocked.

In 2017 the trousers of a Florida defence attorney caught fire during a trial of an accused arsonist. Stephen Gutierrez was arguing that his client's car had spontaneously combusted, when his own trousers burst into flames from electric-cigarette batteries overheating in his pocket.

A single town in China makes over one-third of the world's socks. Datang, known as 'Sock City', in eastern Zhejiang province, is home to over 10,000 separate businesses and mills producing socks and stockings. Every year they churn out 27 billion socks, accounting for 35 per cent of the global market.

In chapter sixteen of *The Natural History*, Pliny the Elder (23/24-79) makes the claim that the Emperor Nero would watch battles in the arena through the soothing hue of translucent emeralds that he held up to his eyes. 'Indeed there is no stone, the colour of which is more delightful to the eye … Neither sunshine, shade nor artificial light effects any change in their appearance; they have always a softened and graduated brilliancy.'

For the earliest sunglasses in a form we'd recognise, we must go back to twelfth-century China and the eyeglasses of smoky quartz crystal known as *Ai Tai* ('dark clouds'), worn not by the fashionable nor the sun-worshipper, but by judges in court to conceal their facial expression.

Tiaras and high heels were first worn by men – 'tiara' is Persian in origin, and originally referred to the colourful peaked headdresses of Persian kings. The earliest known high-heeled shoes also date back to Persia, in the tenth century. Male soldiers on horseback wore them to fix their feet in the stirrups for a secure fighting position in battle. (This also is why American cowboy boots feature a Cuban-type heel.)

In the fourteenth century a rampant craze swept Europe for *crakows*, or *poulaines* – extraordinarily long-toed footwear that tapered to a point. A 2021 study in the *International Journal of Paleopathology* linked this to a huge widespread increase in *hallux valgus* of the big toe, otherwise known as bunions. The impractical shoes were mostly worn by wealthy men keen to exhibit the fact that they had no need to perform manual labour. In 1368 King Charles V (1500-1558), Holy Roman Emperor, passed a law banning *crakows* ('Satan's claws' as they were sometimes called) because they made it difficult for men to kneel in prayer; and in England King Edward IV (1442-1483) banned any shoe with toes longer than 5cm, as he found them too suggestive. The long-toed shoes were said to have been invented by Fulk IV, Count of Anjou (1043-1109), who wore *poulaines* with toes so long that they were fastened to his knees with gold chains, and carved at the extreme point with representations of church windows and birds. Ironically he had them made to hide his hideous bunions.

In 2011 textile conservators discovered that dresses found at the Cistercian convent of Wienhausen in northern Germany had hems lined with medieval manuscripts. The dresses were made by the nuns in the late fifteenth century – not for themselves but for preserving the modesty of the convent's statues.[28]

---

28. Bishop Fulton Sheen (1895-1979) is reputed to have once said: 'Hearing nuns' confessions is like being stoned to death with popcorn.'

In 1998 Karola Baumann, an art teacher from Düsseldorf, noticed that some animals prick up their ears when communicating, and theorised that animals would understand us better if they could see us doing the same. Following this theory she designed and patented a device of mechanical ears that she claimed would allow us to talk with animals. The skullcap with two short 'masts' at either side were fitted with large replicas of animal ears and were operated by remote control kept it a pocket. The ears could move into four positions, Baumann explained, signalling: 'do-what-you-are-told', 'kindness', 'play' and 'love'. Regrettably the invention failed to catch on.

Karola Baumann's animal ear device.

A 'thagomizer' is the name for the cluster of four spikes on the tails of stegosaurian dinosaurs, which we think were wielded by the animals as a defensive weapon against predators. 'Thagomizer' originated not in palaeontology, which had no name for this feature, but with the cartoonist Gary Larson who invented the word in 1982 as part of a joke in his comic strip *The Far Side*. It was then adopted by scientific circles.

The discovery in China of the first preserved dinosaur anus was announced in 2021. The 'cloacal vent' of a *Psittacosaurus*, a Labrador-sized horned relative of the *Triceratops*, was described by palaeontologists as 'perfect' and 'unique'. It even contained fossilised faeces. 'It's like a Swiss Army knife of excretory openings', said Jakob Vinther, a paleobiologist at the University of Bristol in the UK. 'It does everything.'

The first discovered Neanderthal was misidentified as a Cossack. 'Neanderthal 1' was discovered in 1856 submerged under metres of mud in a German cave in the Neander Valley. The palaeontologist August Mayer scoffed at the idea of it being an early human, and instead suggested it was the remains of one of the number of Cossacks who had come to Germany in the early 1800s. From the unusual bone shapes, he said, this one had clearly suffered rickets from poor nutrition as well as arthritis from a lifetime on horseback. The odd-looking skull? The Cossack must have incurred a cranial injury, crawled into the cave and sunk into its mud. All of this made a lot more sense at the time than the outrageous evolutionary theory of Charles Darwin (1809-1882).

Megalosaurus was the first species name applied to an extinct dinosaur. The earliest fossil of the genus is a lower part of a femur found in the seventeenth century. The bone was given to the English naturalist Robert Plot (1640-1696), Professor of Chemistry at the University of Oxford and first curator of the Ashmolean Museum. Plot first declared it to be the thigh bone of a Roman war elephant, only to then decide it belonged to one of the giants mentioned in the Bible.

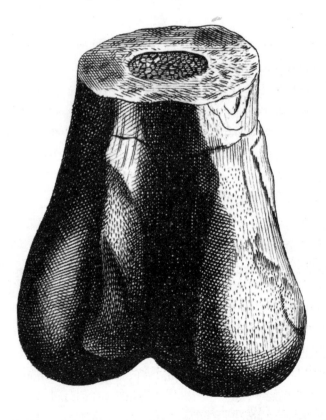

The Megalosaurus *bone. In vol. 5 of* A System of Natural History *by Richard Brookes in 1763 it was labelled* Scrotum humanum, *apparently because of its resemblance to a pair of human testicles.*

Nobody knows why Neanderthals went extinct. In a sense they haven't entirely, as modern Europeans and Asians have around 1-2 per cent Neanderthal DNA. A study of the Neanderthal genome published in May 2023 shows that in particular people with large noses inherit the feature from Neanderthal ancestors, who benefited from oversized honkers to survive the colder Eurasian climate.

Recent archaeological excavations have revealed that Neanderthals wore body glitter, jewellery, makeup and capes.

The earliest evidence of kissing can be found in *Neanderthal Behaviour, Diet and Disease Inferred from Ancient DNA in Dental Calculus*, a paper published in 2017 by a team co-led by Laura Weyrich at Pennsylvania State University. While studying the remains of the last thirteen Neanderthals to walk the Earth, which were found at El Sidrón in northwest Spain, Weyrich was surprised to find that she recognised the genetic signature of a microorganism on one of the teeth – *Methanobrevibacter oralis*, which is also found in the mouths of modern humans. By comparing the Neanderthal strain with the modern strain, she was able to estimate that the microorganism transferred between Neanderthals and *Homo sapiens* roughly 120,000 years ago. This being a period when the two were interbreeding, a likely route for this transfer was kissing. 'When you kiss someone, oral microbes will go back and forth between your mouths,' Weyrich says. 'It could have happened once and then propagated … But it could also be something that occurred more regularly.'

There has never been such a thing as a 'sabre-toothed tiger'. The smilodon, to which this label was applied, was more closely related to marsupials than it was to tigers or cats.

There were, however, such things as sabre-toothed anchovies. Researcher Alessio Capobianco and his colleagues discovered that such creatures evolved following the destruction of the dinosaurs, killing off many of the oceans' predators. Microcomputed tomography was used to study two fossilised fish that lived about 55 million years ago, one found in Belgium and the other in Pakistan. Both were similar to modern anchovies except for the fact that both had one long sabrelike tooth at the front of the mouth and were 1m long. 'I would love to know what sabre-toothed anchovies tasted like – they probably would taste different because they ate other fishes instead of plankton,' said Capobianco.

Sharks are older than trees. Fossil evidence for sharks goes back as far as 450 million years ago, though no dental samples have been found from this era, suggesting they were originally toothless.[29] It's thought that the depth and diversity of environments to which sharks can adapt allowed them to survive ocean change and catastrophic surface events. Some 30 million years later the first plant life invaded land.

---

29. At 450 million years old, this also makes sharks older than the rings of Jupiter, which only formed a paltry million years ago or so, and even older than Saturn's rings, which formed no more than 400 million years ago.

The youngest known species on Earth is at most eighty-nine years old and eats only nylon. *Paenarthrobacter ureafaciens KI72* is a species of bacteria that was discovered living in ponds of wastewater from a nylon factory by Japanese scientists in 1975. The bacteria have a unique set of enzymes that allow them to eat nylon but nothing else, which means they can only have existed after the invention of nylon in 1935 – making them the same age as Dame Judi Dench.

The 'longest animal in the world' is a disputed title. The two contenders are the lion's mane jellyfish (*Cyanea capillata*), the largest recorded specimen of which had tentacles measured at 36.6m in length. The other is a bootlace worm (*Lineus longissimus*) that was found in 1864 washed up on the coast of Fife, UK, recorded as 55m long. However, bootlace worms can stretch to several times their actual length, and it's possible this was true of the 1864 specimen.

A pod of killer whales sleeps by forming a tight circle and synchronising their breathing and movements as one. They take breaths together and then submerge before resurfacing a while later. This synchronicity is unlike anything else in the animal kingdom.

Seals and sea lions have retractable nipples that retreat into the body when offspring don't need feeding.

The baculum, or penis bone, of the walrus is around 1m long. The Inuit people made clubs from walrus penis bones, and windows from the penis skin and stomach linings. In 1994 the Republican Congressman Don Young caused a stir when he suggestively waggled a giant baculum during the testimony of Mollie Beattie, the first woman to lead US Fish and Wildlife Service during a congressional hearing. 'This is my gavel,' he explained to the Alaska television station KTVA, 'it's made out of a walrus penis.'

Goldfish and the related crucian carp can survive for months without oxygen at the bottom of ice-covered ponds.

Fish can get seasick. This was discovered by Stuttgart zoologist Dr Reinhold Hilbig in 2009, after sending forty-nine fish in a tank up in a plane that made a steep dive, to simulate the effect of weightlessness in space. Hilbig studied the fish and noted that 'they lost their balance, behaving like humans who get seasick. They lost their orientation, became confused and looked as if they were about to vomit.'

The Italian poet Gabriele D'Annunzio (1863-1938) had his books printed on rubber so that he could read them while lazing in the enormous sunken tile bath that he shared with his goldfish.[30]

---

30. The grand bath was but the smallest of extravagances at D'Annunzio's Vittoriale degli italiani estate overlooking Lake Garda. Elsewhere in the gardens are the plane that he flew for a pamphleteering run over Vienna during the First World War, a large naval vessel he used to taunt the Austrians in a raid in 1918, and the enormous bow section of the 88m- (290ft-) long navy cruiser *The Puglia*, which was hauled up the hill and placed in the woods behind the house – a gift from Benito Mussolini (1883-1945).

Fish fart to communicate. In 2003 biologists investigating a mysterious underwater sound realised it was caused by bubbles exiting a herring's anus. No fish had ever been known before to make sounds from its anus. 'It sounds just like a high-pitched raspberry,' said Ben Wilson of the University of British Columbia in Vancouver, Canada. They christened the noise Fast Repetitive Tick (FRT).

Parrotfish eat coral and excrete it as sand. It's estimated that as much as 70 per cent of the white sandy beaches of the Caribbean and Hawaii are made of sand excreted by parrotfish. A single large adult parrotfish can excrete over a tonne of sand in one year.

The tripodfish (*Bathypterois grallator*) has three rigid fin 'legs' that it uses to stand on the bottom of the ocean and kick approaching prey into its mouth.

A number of species of fish can walk on land. Mudskippers grow up to 30cm long and are probably the fish most adept at walking, able to spend several days out of water to cross land and even can climb mangroves. Their side pectoral fins are jointed and located more forward and under their elongated body, which allows them to crawl, skip, climb and leap distances of 60cm with the use of their tail. The climbing gourami, or climbing perch, is able to breathe atmospheric oxygen, and 'walks' on land by resting on its gill plates and using its fins and tails to push itself along.

An illustration of an Indonesian four-legged running fish (*Poisson courant*) that was said to have followed its discoverer around 'like a little dog'. From Louis Renard's *Fishes, Crayfishes, and Crabs …* (1719), a wildly imaginative 'survey' of Indonesian aquatic life.

The mangrove killifish of the western Atlantic is the only fish that lives in trees. It can survive for months out of the water and isn't preoccupied with finding a mate in these difficult and remote situations, because it doesn't need one. It's the only known hermaphrodite vertebrate that is self-fertilising.

Female blanket octopuses are named after their shimmering, iridescent, capelike flesh, reaching lengths of up to 2m. The females can be up to 40,000 times heavier than the males, who are about the size of a walnut and have no cape.

Female market squid don't have the size advantage of the female blanket octopus over their males, so instead they counter unwanted advances by displaying fake testicles. By activating white stripes of reflective leucophore cells on their body, in the same area where males have white testes, they disguise their sex to go unnoticed.

Some snails fire 'love darts' at each other, effectively harpooning potential partners. The gypsobelum is a hard, pointed dart that is formed and stored internally in a dart sac in sexually mature slugs and snails. Before copulation, the two snails (or slugs) approach each other and 'shoot' each other close-range in a stabbing action into their flesh. It has nothing to do with the exchange of sperm, which is done separately, but the dart is coated in mucus that helps with reproduction.

The Maya used wasp and hornet nests as booby traps against invaders of their citadels. According to the *Popol Vuh* ('Book of the People'): 'They were like clouds of smoke when they came out of each of the gourds. The warriors were thus finished off because of the insects.'

Bumblebees trigger flowers to explosively release pollen by unhinging their wings and vibrating their bodies in the tone of middle C.

If a male honeybee is successful in mating, he releases semen so forcefully that there's an audible pop as all the blood from his body rushes to his endophallus (the bee equivalent of a penis) causing it to explode, and he falls to the ground paralysed.

Researchers at Nottingham Trent University found in 2017 that honeybees let out a 'whoop' sound of surprise every time they bump into each other inside the hive.

British bees almost died out entirely in the first quarter of the twentieth century due to a pernicious mite. Stocks were replenished with Dutch bees and Italian queens.

Daniel Wildman (*fl.*1771) was a London beekeeper and honey vendor who publicised his shop by riding a horse standing up on the saddle while wearing a beard of bees. Patty Astley (1741-1803), wife of Philip Astley the founder of the modern circus, also performed an equestrian act in which she wore a 'muff' of bees around her hands and arms.

Not only is spider silk stronger and more durable than steel, but some spiders, like the European garden spider (*Araneus diadematus*), can produce up to seven different kinds of silks depending on what they're needed for.

There's a species of Australian wasp called *Aha ha*. Entomologist Arnold Menke explained how he named it in 1977 after opening a package full of specimens and shouting 'Aha!', to which a colleague sceptically replied 'ha'. Menke went on to make his car's licence plate 'AHA HA'.

In 1995 scientists at NASA's Marshall Space Flight Center in Alabama exposed spiders to a variety of drugs to gauge their effects, which they were able to see from the styles of web the arachnids spun while under the influence.

Clockwise left to right: No drugs, marijuana, chloral hydrate, mescaline, caffeine, Benzedrine.

Scientists aboard a British research ship exploring hydrothermal vents outside Antarctica in 2011 discovered a new type of yeti crab that had lustrously thick, hairlike bristles on its chest and arms. They named it the Hoff crab, after David Hasselhoff.

The glorious blond head scales of the *Neopalpa Donaldtrumpi*, an orange-yellow moth of Mexican origin with unusually small genitalia structures, named after Donald Trump in 2017 by the Iranian-Canadian scientist Vazrick Nazari.

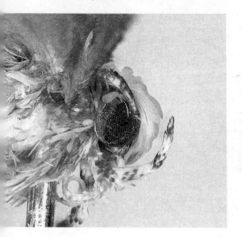

Agathidium vaderi is a slime mould named after Darth Vader. Other *Agathidium* slime moulds with famous namesakes include *A. bushi* (George Bush), *A. cheneyi* (Dick Cheney) and *A. rumsfeldi* (Donald Rumsfeld).[31]

Pieza is a genus of flies found in the Americas and the West Indies. There are eleven wittily named species, including *Pieza pi*, *Pieza rhea*, *Pieza kake* and *Pieza deresistans*.

31. Slime moulds are not to be underestimated. The single-celled amoebae can remember, make decisions and anticipate change – *Physarum polycephalum* in particular has been found to solve mazes, imitate the layout of man-made transportation networks, and select the healthiest food option from a wide-ranging menu, displaying intelligence despite not having a brain nor nervous system.

In 2023 Harrison Ford had a newly discovered species of snake in Peru's Andes mountains named after him. *Tachymenoides harrisonfordi* joins an ant (*Pheidole harrisonfordi*) and a spider (*Calponia harrisonfordi*) named after the actor. 'These scientists keep naming critters after me, but it's always the ones that terrify children,' Ford said in response. 'I don't understand. I spend my free time cross-stitching. I sing lullabies to my basil plants, so they won't fear the night.'

In 2014 a pine tree planted in a Los Angeles park in memory of George Harrison (1943-2001) was destroyed by beetles.

Almost 40 per cent of all described insects, and 25 per cent of all known animal species, are beetles.[32]

The eye of the dragonfly is an astounding piece of natural technology. While humans have one lens per eye, dragonflies have thousands of miniature lenses called ommatidia, which allow it to have a 360-degree field of vision and even see directly behind itself.

In 1996, in the British village of Stokeinteignhead, Devon, a resident named Neil Simmons would go out into his garden at night to hoot at owls, until finally one evening an owl hooted a reply. This became a nightly repartee for over a year, until Mr Simmons discovered that he had been communicating with his neighbour Fred Cornes, who had been as equally delighted to strike up a conversation with an owl.

---

32. In London's Natural History Museum, beetle specimens fill 22,000 drawers.

The Salmin Brothers of Padua, Italy, worked with a team of engineers to invent a microscopic typeface they called carattere a occhio di mosca ('fly's-eye'). The type was so achingly small that it physically damaged the eyesight of its compositor, Giuseppe Geche, and others involved in its printing.

A woodpecker's tongue is wrapped around its skull. A flamingo's tongue has erectile tissue similar to a penis: when eating, the tissue fills with blood and stiffens to help stabilise its head. A Komodo dragon can use its tongue to detect prey 4km away.

A 2016 study by the universities of Houston and Vienna found that ravens can have paranoid thoughts – a level of abstract thinking that was previously thought to be unique to humans.

Australian musk ducks have the ability to mimic human speech. This was discovered only in the 1980s, when a four-year-old duck named Ripper at Tidbinbilla Nature Reserve was recorded by researcher Dr Peter Fullagar imitating speech and making other vocalisations. Ripper would mimic the sound of a door slamming shut, and occasionally scream 'You bloody fool!' during 'aggressive mating displays'. The 1980s recordings had lain undiscovered until 2021. Other cases were noted by the researchers: one duck in Pensthorpe

Natural Park, UK, was heard 'coughing and [mimicking] a snorting pony'; while another at Slimbridge Wildfowl Trust had been seen making 'the characteristic cough of his bird keeper and also of a squeak of a turnstile'.

Writing in his *Historia Animalium*, Aristotle (384-322 BC) says that the parrot 'is said to be human-tongued, and it becomes even more outrageous after drinking wine'.

Advertisement from *Le Figaro*, 1881: 'WANTED – a professor to come twice a week to the house of a noble family in order to reform the pronunciation of a parrot.'

A proposed pistol-powered solution for vermin problems, designed by J. A. Williams in 1882.

In 2016 scientists discovered that rats can laugh when they tickled their bellies and recorded them giggling at a frequency too high for the human ear to pick up. Michael Brecht at Humboldt University of Berlin, Germany, also found that rats love to play hide-and-seek.

Squirrels and other rodents are responsible for 10-20 per cent of all power outages in the USA, according to *The Washington Post*.

In ancient Persia the otter was held sacred by the Zoroastrian people, who classified the killing of the creature as a heinous crime and would even bury with ceremony any dead otter they came across. There were eighteen punishments for the man found guilty of lutracide (murder of 'the water-dog'), which included being forced to atone by killing 10,000 corpse-flies, 10,000 frogs, 10,000 snakes and 10,000 worms. Other reparations included carrying 10,000 loads of wood to the sacred fire, and relinquishing land and property – including any daughters – to 'godly men'.

In 1996 the Swedish Engineering Science Academy concluded that of the more than 6000 reports of possible foreign submarine activity noted by the Swedish Navy between 1981 and 1994, there was evidence for only six incidents. In particular they found that forty of the incidents between 1992 and 1994 were not enemy submarine propellers but swimming mink or otters, which can produce the same readings.

The upper shell of turtles and tortoises is actually their ribcage –
each rib fuses together after emerging from the spine and grows
around the shoulders and pelvis of the animal to form a single
carapace. The underside of the shell is a different piece grown from
the shoulder girdle and sternum (breastbone). So to say that turtles
'live inside' their shells is like saying you live inside your rib cage.

Cats can technically be classified as a liquid as well as a solid – this
according to the paper *On the Rheology of Cats* published in 2014 by
Marc-Antoine Fardin of the Paris Diderot University. The physicist
demonstrates that, with their ability to fill the small containers they
habitually jump into, cats fit the necessary criteria of liquids.

The earliest named cat was *Nedjem*, an Egyptian pet feline of the
fifteenth century BC depicted on the tomb of Puimre, second priest of
Amun during the reign of Queen Hatshepsut. *Nedjem* means 'Sweetie'.

The vast majority of cats shouldn't be given milk –
they're lactose intolerant.

The first female to circumnavigate the globe was a milk-goat with
no name but was celebrated on her return to London as 'The Well-
Travelled Goat'. She served under Lieutenant James Cook (1728-
1779) on board HMS *Endeavour* on his voyage of 1768-1771.

Emperor Wudi (236-290), the first Emperor of China, reportedly gathered so many beautiful women for his pleasure in the palace that he couldn't choose which one to spend the night with. He would ride past them in a cart pulled by a goat, and whomever the goat stopped in front of would be his chosen concubine for the evening.

US President Calvin Coolidge (1872-1933) had two pet lions called Tax Reduction and Budget Bureau, a pygmy hippo called William Johnson Hippopotamus, and a raccoon called Rebecca that he adopted as a pet after refusing to eat her as an alternative to turkey at Thanksgiving.

US President Theodore Roosevelt's daughter Alice (1894-1980) kept a snake in the White House called Emily Spinach.

Thomas Hardy (1840-1928) had a pet cat called Kiddleywinkempoops.

Prince Rupert of the Rhine (1619-1682) had a white hunting poodle called Boy that was rumoured to be a dog-witch, and would cock his leg whenever he heard the name of John Pym (1584-1643), the leader of the Parliamentarian forces. Boy would charge with his master into battle and was killed at the Battle of Marston Moor on 2 July 1644.

Some Rottweilers purr like cats when they're happy.

Camels were employed as lawnmowers at London Zoo, like this one ridden by gardener Fred Perry in 1913. When horses were used to pull early mowers, the animals were sometimes fitted with leather boots to protect the lawn. The camel was best suited to the job, as its hooves didn't leave prints in the grass.[33]

Camels have three sets of eyelids, can close their nostrils completely to keep sand out in high winds, and can produce urine as thick as syrup.

Koalas have fingerprints almost indistinguishable from those of humans.

33. When Edwin Beard Budding (1796-1846) invented the lawnmower in 1830, he was so worried that a neighbour might see him using the strange machine and report him as mad that he tested his invention at night.

Fingerprints, sometimes called 'chanced impressions', are formed by the friction from touching the walls of our mother's womb. By week nineteen they're set. This is why prints are truly unique to every person, even for genetically identical twins.

The Museo delle Anime del Purgatorio, Rome, houses scorched artefacts that are claimed to have been touched by the burning souls of purgatory.

You can fingerprint an Egyptian mummy.

The swirls in our fingerprints have been shown to correlate with high likelihood of conditions including asthma, autism, diabetes, gastrointestinal cancers, infertility, periodontitis and schizophrenia.

The star attractions of Pyongyang Central Zoo in North Korea are listed as a cigarette-smoking chimpanzee called Azalea, basketball-playing monkeys, and a dog who is trained to use an abacus.

The first European depiction of an orangutan, from Daniel
Beeckman's *To and From the Island of Borneo* (1718).

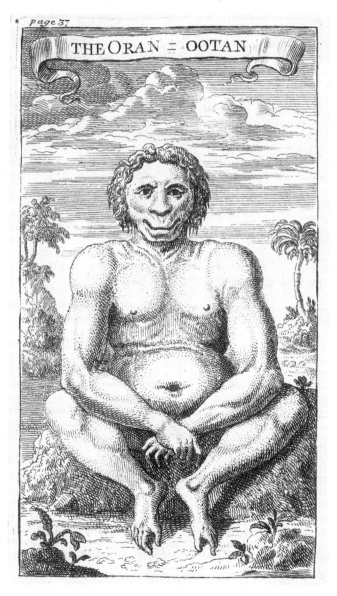

During filming of *Star Wars: Episode VI – Return of the Jedi* (1983), when wearing his Chewbacca costume on location in the forests of California, the actor Peter Mayhew (1944-2019) had to be accompanied by a security team in high-visibility jackets. The concern was that hunters would mistake him for Bigfoot and take a potshot at him.

On 30 November 1959 the American Embassy in Kathmandu issued an official memo on what to do when the Yeti, or Abominable Snowman, is found. Titled 'Regulations Governing Mountain Climbing Expeditions in Nepal – Relating to Yeti', the memo instructs that yeti hunters should pay 5000 rupees to the government of Nepal for a permit. If the Yeti is found, the government should be notified, not the news media. The creature can be photographed or caught alive, but only killed in 'an emergency arising out of self-defence'.

Something you've probably always fretted about is what to do if you encounter a yeti, or *Migoi* as the locals call it. According to the Bhutanese writer Tshering Tashi, it depends on which gender of yeti you meet. If you're approached by a male, then it's best to run uphill as it's so hirsute that it'll trip on its body hair. If you're chased by a female, the standard advice is to run downhill, as it will be slowed down by its large sagging breasts.

This should only really be helpful if you're wandering Bigfoot Valley in Sakteng Wildlife Sanctuary, which is 750sq. km of conservation area set aside by the Bhutanese for the protection of the yeti.

Visitors to Paris's Gallery of Palaeontology and Comparative Anatomy are greeted in the foyer with the sight of Emmanuel Frémiet's (1824-1910) terrifying sculpture *Orangutan Strangling a Borneo Savage* (1895).

The Bigorne is a creature of French folklore in Anjou, Normandy and Auvergne. The fat, panther-cow monster with a human face fed exclusively on men who obey their wives. (Its obesity represents just how many such men there were.) The Bigorne is usually accompanied by a sickly thin creature known as Chicheface, who feeds on obedient wives, hence his starvation.

The 'Bigorne' (right) and the Chicheface (left).

♀♂

Worship of the ancient Greek goddess Aphrodite was active in the twentieth century – not in Greece, however, but Long Island, New York, USA. The Church of Aphrodite was founded in 1939 by Gleb Botkin (1900-1969), a Russian émigré and son of Dr Yevgeny Botkin, the Russian court physician who was murdered at Yekaterinburg by the Bolsheviks with Tsar Nicholas II and his family on 17 July 1918. Botkin believed that it was the patriarchy that was to blame for all the issues plaguing mankind. 'Men!' he once cried. 'Just look at the mess we've made!'

♀♂

In 2021 it was reported that Juan Carlos I, King of Spain 1975-2014, had so many extra-marital affairs, allegedly fathering two children (sovereign immunity protected him from paternity suits), that the Spanish Secret Service covertly reduced his sex drive. Former police official José Manuel Villarejo testified that the King was secretly dosed with female hormones and testosterone inhibitors because his libido was seen as a 'problem for the state'.

♀♂

In the eighteenth century when a Corsican husband died, his widow's first action was to gather the other local women and toss his corpse up and down on a blanket, in order to see if he was playing dead to escape the marriage. This was reported by Dr Johann August Unzer (1727-1799), editor of the medical weekly *Der Arzt. Eine medicinische Wochenschrift*, who claimed the blanket tossing often went on for hours, and that it occasionally 'recalled to life' the man 'who to all appearance had been dead'. His desperate bid for freedom foiled, he was left to the mercy of his former widow.

♀♂

When J. W. C. van Gorcum, a colonel of the Dutch Cavalry and militia commissioner in Limburg, died in 1880 after thirty-eight years of marriage, he was buried in the Protestant cemetery of the town in a tomb pressed against the perimeter wall. When his wife, J. C. P. H. van Aefferden, a Catholic, died eight years later, she left instructions to refuse her interment in the family tomb. Instead, she requested to be buried in a monument against the perimeter wall of the Catholic cemetery, directly against her husband's tomb on the Protestant side, and have their resting places joined by the clasped hands shown in this photograph.

The tombs of J. W. C. van Gorcum and his wife J. C. P. H. van Aefferden.

♀♂

The sign for the female sex ♀ originates in the Greek shorthand symbol for phosphorus, while the male symbol ♂ is derived from the iron symbol. The Greeks associated metals with the planets: Venus (*Phosphorus*) was associated with copper, the relatively soft metal that can turn green; while Mars (*Thouros*) was linked with iron, the harder red metal used to fashion weapons.

♀♂

Thousands of these metal badges survive in Europe from the Middle Ages, worn by Christians on pilgrimage. They commonly feature animated vulvas and penises performing actions like climbing ladders, wearing hats and riding horses. The example shown here is known in the scholarship as *Pussy Goes a Hunting*. Very little contemporary literature mentions these early souvenirs, and so their meaning is mysterious. Probably symbolising fertility, it has also been suggested that they were used to ward off evil, or perhaps to signify availability for sexual encounters.

♀♂

From around 1100 until 1797 the doge of Venice would ceremonially marry the Adriatic Sea every year, ritually throwing a golden ring into its waters. The Marriage of the Sea ceremony, which took place every Ascension Day, was revived in 1965.

♀♂

In March 2018 two women of Fort Meyers, Florida, married a giant fig tree in Snell Family Park, in the hope that it would prevent city officials from going ahead with their plan to cut it down. 'If they cut down this tree, we're going to be widows,' they claimed. The plan worked.

Every English elm tree of today is descended from a single tree transported by the Romans from Italy to Britain, via the Iberian peninsula, in order to support and train vines.

♀♂

Toronto in 1926 was the scene of 'The Great Stork Derby' as it was called in the papers, when financier Charles Vance Millar (1854-1926) died and left instructions that his fortune be left to the woman who gave birth to the most children in the next decade. Ten years later the results were a tie, with four women producing nine living children each. Each woman received $125,000.

♀♂

The One-Two-Two, named after its address of 122 Rue de Provence, eighth arrondissement, was one of the most luxurious brothels of Paris between 1924 and 1946. Each of its rooms had a different theme as part of a 'journey around the world'. This included a pirate room, in which the occupants made use of a four-poster bed that would rock like a boat in a storm while jets of water would drench them; a medieval torture chamber with chains and whips; and a replica of an Orient Express train cabin, where for an additional fee you could be joined by the conductor.

♀♂

The entire world's supply of Viagra and Botox is made in Ireland.

For one day in 2015, Ireland inadvertently legalised all illicit drugs including ecstasy, meth and ketamine when the 1977 Misuse of Drugs Act was deemed to be unconstitutional by the Irish Court of Appeal. Some 24 hours later emergency legislation was swiftly enacted to restore the prohibition.

Pope Paul II (1417-1471) and German Emperor Frederick III (1831-1888) are thought to have died from overdoses of melon.

The Language of Stamps – Victorian lovers communicated secretly by positioning the stamp on their letter in various meaningful ways.

Happiness can give you a heart attack. The surprise finding came from a 2016 University Hospital Zurich study of people with *takotsubo* syndrome, otherwise known as 'broken heart syndrome'. This is when the left ventricle can suddenly balloon and distort to the shape of the *takotsubo* pot used to catch octopuses in Japan, causing pain, breathlessness and occasionally death. Originally it was associated with stress caused by negative emotions, but the researchers found that sudden bursts of joy can be lethal, too.[34]

---

34. Have a great day, everyone.

SOME NOTABLE FIGURES BURIED
WITHOUT THEIR HEART

Henry I (*c.*1068-1135)

Richard I (1157-1199)

Eleanor of Castile (1241-1290)

Robert the Bruce (1274-1329)

John II Casimir Vasa, King of Poland (1609-1672)

Napoleon I (1769-1821)

Percy Bysshe Shelley (1792-1822)

Peter I of Brazil and **Dom Pedro IV of Portugal** (1798-1834)

Frédéric Chopin (1810-1849)
had his heart pickled in brandy, sent to Poland
and set into a church pillar.

Thomas Hardy (1840-1928)
legend has it that a cat ate his heart the night before
its scheduled burial with his first wife, Emma.

Tsar Boris III of Bulgaria (1894-1943)

Thirty bishops of Würzburg
had their hearts buried at the Ebrach monastery.

The Herzgruft ('Heart Crypt')
in Vienna holds fifty-four hearts of members
of the House of Habsburg.

Dead bodies can get goosebumps. As part of rigor mortis, tiny muscles in the skin called arrector pili flex and make hair follicles rise. Some (living) people can also give themselves goosebumps on command. It's called voluntarily generated piloerection (VGP), and according to neurophysiologists it shouldn't be possible.

Australia's first camel accidentally shot and killed its owner. John Ainsworth Horrocks (1818-1846), founder of the town of Penwortham, set out in 1846 on a mission to explore the Australian interior. His steed for the journey was Harry, the only survivor of the first shipment of camels to arrive in the country to serve as pack animals. During the expedition Horrocks saw a bird he wished to shoot, and hastily began to change ammunition. Harry the camel stepped to one side, jogging the shotgun trigger and blasting Horrocks, who lost a finger, part of his cheek and some teeth. By the time other members of his party got him to a doctor he had died of his wounds.

On 4 June 1923 an American jockey named Frank Hayes won a steeplechase at Belmont Park racetrack in Elmont, New York, despite never having won a race before and also being dead. During the race he had suffered a fatal heart attack but his horse, Sweet Kiss, kept going and won by a head.

The official entry for English scholar Obadiah Walker (1616-1699) in the prestigious *Oxford Dictionary of National Biography* ends with the sentence 'His ghost is reputed to haunt staircase 8 of University College'.

SOME BOOKS WRITTEN BY GHOSTS

According to *Essential Cataloguing: The Basics* by J. H. Bowman (2002), the authoritative guide followed by the British Library and the American Librarian Association, books written by the ghosts of authors must be catalogued under the name of the post-mortem personality, not the name of the medium who channelled and recorded the work. This means, for example, that technically speaking Shakespeare's final work was not *The Two Noble Kinsmen* (1613-1614) but *For Jesus' Sake – By Shakespeare's Spirit* (1920). You can find it catalogued under 'Shakespeare, William (Spirit)'. Others include:

Part Second of the Mystery of Edwin Drood (1873) by the Spirit Pen of Charles Dickens

Jap Herron: A Novel Written from the Ouija Board (1917) written by Mark Twain seven years after his death, helped by Emily Grant Hutchings

Autobiography by Jesus of Nazareth (1884) by 'humble instrument' Olive Pettis

The Great Mystery of Life Beyond Death (1983) by a deceased Sir Arthur Conan Doyle (1859-1930)

The Post-Mortem Journal of T. E. Lawrence (1964) 'recorded through automatic writing by Jane Sherwood'

Psychic Messages from Oscar Wilde (1934), edited by Hester Travers Smith

The outlaw George Parrott (1834-1881), aka Big Nose George, aka Big Beak Parrott, holds the distinction of being the only American turned into a pair of shoes. Following his capture the highwayman was hanged, and his body was taken by Dr John Osborne who had the local tanner use his skin to make a pair of shoes and a medicine bag. Osborne would go on to be the first Democratic Governor of Wyoming, and reputedly wore the shoes at his inaugural ball in 1893.

Reported in the *Edinburgh Evening News*, 18 August 1978:

> While they were waiting at a bus stop in Clermiston, Mr and Mrs Daniel Thirsty were threatened by Mr Robert Clear. 'He demanded that I give him my wife's purse', said Mr Thirsty. 'Telling him that the purse was in her basket, I bent down, put my hands up her skirt, detached her artificial leg and hit him over the head with it. It was not my intention to do anything more than frighten him off, but unhappily for us all he died.'

The Dutch once ate their prime minister. Johan de Witt (1625-1672) was the elected Grand Pensionary of Holland, in control of the Dutch political system from 1653 until the *Rampjaar* ('Disaster Year') of 1672, when an alliance of France, England and some German states easily invaded the Dutch republic. The Dutch people blamed the invasion on De Witt and his brother Cornelis for their neglect of the Dutch States Army, and a furious mob made up of the Hague's civic militia seized and shot the De Witt brothers. Their naked bodies were hung from the public gibbet, while an Orangist mob cut out and roasted body parts including their livers and ate them in a cannibalistic frenzy.

SOME NOTABLE DEFENESTRATIONS

Prague leads the way when it comes to throwing people out of the window. The Defenestrations of Prague refers to two separate incidents. In 1419 a Hussite mob ejected a judge, the burgomaster and around thirteen members of the town council through the windows of the New Town Hall, which led to the Hussite War that lasted until 1436. Nearly two hundred years later, in 1618, two governors and their secretary were thrown from the 20m-high windows of Prague Castle, which sparked the Thirty Years' War.

In 1562 Akbar the Great (1542-1605), third Mughal Emperor, defenestrated his general and foster brother Adham Khan from Agra Fort for murdering a rival. Khan survived with broken legs, so Akbar had him brought up and thrown out again – this time killing him.

Another self-defenestration was carried out accidentally on 9 July 1993 when Garry Hoy, thirty-eight, of the Canadian law firm Holden Day Wilson, fell from the twenty-fourth floor of the Toronto-Dominion Centre. In an effort to demonstrate to a group of visiting students that his office windows were 'unbreakable' he had thrown himself against the glass, which indeed did not break, but unfortunately did pop out of its frame.

On 27 October 1997 the US basketball player Charles Barkley tossed a man through a plate-glass window of a nightclub, after the man threw a glass of ice at him. 'He lifted that kid up and flung him like he was a toy,' a witness told *The New York Times*. 'If you bother me, I'm going to whip your ass,' explained Barkley.

Books also have their own history of notable defenestrations. The enormous *Codex Gigas* mentioned on page 47 was once thrown out of a fourth-floor window at Stockholm Castle to save it from a fire that broke out. Luckily, the 74.8kg book's fall was broken by it landing squarely on an oblivious passer. Similarly, on the night of 3 February 1731 the Royal Palace of Brussels erupted in flames, and its librarians began frantically throwing books out of the window to save them. One onlooker was reported to have been killed by a particularly hefty flying folio. And in a curious modern update of the tradition, in 2015 Glenn Pladsen of Boulder, Colorado, USA, was ticketed by police for throwing a book out of the window of his moving car onto the highway. It was later learned that Mr Padsen was the long-sought 'book tosser of Boulder' and had disposed of some 600 books this way around town. His excuse was that he didn't know what else to do with them.

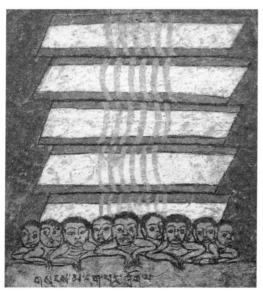

A Buddhist card warning of a realm of hell in which monks who don't keep up with their studies will be crushed under enormous books.

☪

A legendary tree of the Chilean island of Chiloé, which was reported to grow in the shape of Jesus on the Cross. From *Descripcion historial archipielago de Chiloé* ... (1791) by Father Pedro Gonzalez de Agüeros.

Verdadera Efigie del Arbol que en figura de Cruz, y Cruci-fixo se halló en el Valle de Limache, Reino de Chile año de 1636

F Vyena f

☩☥

On its publication, Christoph Luxenberg's book *The Syro-Aramaic Reading of the Koran* (2007) caused a sensation among scholars with knowledge of Semitic languages, with the demonstration that many puzzling aspects of the Qur'an are solved if certain words are read as Syriac and not Arabic. One fascinating example of how the translation changes is with the mentions of the wide-eyed *houris*, the willing virgins promised to the faithful in suras XLIV.54; LII.20, LV.72, and LVI.22. Luxenberg points to how in Syriac, the word *hur* is a feminine plural adjective meaning 'white', with the word 'raisin' implicitly understood. Therefore the *houris* that martyrs expect to receive in paradise might not be seventy-two virgins, but seventy-two 'white raisins' of 'crystal clarity'. Luxenberg points to the context clearly suggesting that it is food and drink that is on offer, not women.

☩☥

Jannah, the Islamic paradise, is a landscape of titanic, magical flora that offers cool shade and endless fruit. (One tradition reports that, when the trees knock against each other, they strike a beautiful note like giant bells.) The colossal and mysterious Sidrat al-Muntahā ('Lote-Tree of the Utmost Farthest Boundary') looms at the far end of Jannah, near the abode of Allah himself (Qur'an 53:20), marking the boundary of Heaven, a border that no creation can cross. There is also the enormous tree known as Ṭūbā ('Blessedness'), a term mentioned only once in the Qur'an but again in the Hadiths, that over the years inspired writers like Sohrevardi (1154-1191) to suggest it to be a tree in Heaven where the mythical bird Simurgh (equivalent to a griffin) lay its eggs. Abu Hurairah (*c.*603-*c.*679) reports Muhammad as saying: 'In paradise, there is a tree under the shadow of which a rider can travel for a hundred years.'

A *Goodly Company* (1933) is the work of a London-based artist and spirit medium Constance 'Ethel' Le Rossignol (1873-1970), a former First World War nurse, who was awarded the British War Medal and the Victory Medal. Between 1920 and 1933, she produced a series of forty-four dazzling paintings of the spirit world, or as she calls it the 'Sphere of Spirit', based on visions she credits to a spirit known only to her as J. P. F. One reviewer compared her to 'William Blake at his mystical maddest'.

Constance 'Ethel' Le Rossignol's vision of the afterlife from A Goodly Company *(1933) as channelled through a spirit guide. 'This sequence of designs is shown to open the eyes of all men to the glorious world of spiritual power which lies about them,' she wrote.*

Less than half of Leonardo da Vinci's *The Last Supper*, c.1495-1498, survives. Its deterioration was noted soon after its completion. By using paints of an ephemeral nature on a thin exterior wall, humidity swiftly ravaged the masterpiece. 'The painting is all but ruined,' lamented Gian Paulo Lomazzo in the second half of the sixteenth century. Major, and often compromising, restorations have been conducted since 1726, and the result is that today, like a sinking ship of Theseus, just 42.5 per cent of *The Last Supper* is Leonardo's work; 17.5 per cent is lost. The remaining 40 per cent is the work of restorers. Frankly, it's astonishing that any original detail remains at all. In 1652 workmen sliced off Christ's feet while installing a doorway in the wall. Napoleon's soldiers reportedly threw bricks at the apostles' heads. A bomb nearly destroyed it on 16 August 1943; and the air pollution of post-war Milan coupled with the effects of crowds of tourists have been detrimental ever since.

Such is the impermanence of artists' colours that, for example, it means no one alive today has ever seen a painting by J. M. W. Turner (1775-1851) in its original intended state. Many of the bright pigments he used in his works were known at the time to quickly fade – they're referred to as 'fugitive colours'. Carmine-red is particularly elusive – in the Turner work *Waves Breaking against the Wind* (c.1840) it was used to paint the last colours of the sun striking the clouds, but today it has faded to a grey, completely changing the tone of the work. Turner was aware of this, and had a reputation for treating his work poorly, keeping paintings stacked in damp corners (where mould flourished on the egg-based primer). He even tore a hole in a corner of one masterpiece to form a cat flap for his seven Manx cats.

The exuberant Tyrian purple was first used by the Phoenicians as early as 1570BC and was prized for its resistance to fading – it actually brightens with sun exposure. And where was this chemical found? In the mucus secretion of a predatory sea snail of the eastern Mediterranean Sea. Royal blue was also extracted from a similar marine snail.

In the nineteenth century molluscs were no longer a practical option for sourcing purple dye on a mass scale. An alternative appeared in the form of the dye mauve, which was accidentally created in 1856 by a nineteen-year-old Londoner named William Perkin (1838-1907), while attempting to synthesise quinine from coal tar in the home laboratory he'd set up in his parents' loft. Perkin's method for making purple was instantly preferable to the alternative source at the time. This was a substance called murexide, which was named after the murex snail in honour of Tyrian purple, but was, in fact, bird excrement.

Known as 'mommia', 'mummy', 'Egyptian brown' and most revealingly *caput mortuum* ('dead man's head'), the tarry brown pigment popular with artists in the nineteenth century was sourced from the most gruesome of means: by grinding up the desiccated corpses of ancient Egyptians, as well as, at one point in its history, mummies of the Guanche people of the Canary Islands and, during shortages, the corpses of slaves and executed criminals. Traditionally mixed with white pitch and myrrh, recipes for its concoction vary – some advise pulverising the whole corpse, while others call for using 'only the finest muscle'. This tarry brown pigment had no use as a watercolour, but was excellent for dark shading, and enjoyed popularity in Europe from the sixteenth to – astonishingly – the early twentieth century, despite its tendency to crack and react with other colours due to its ingredients of ammonia and fat.

Pigeons can tell the difference between a Monet and a Picasso. In 1995 a Japanese research team led by Shigeru Watanabe of Tokyo's Keio University successfully trained the birds to differentiate between work by the impressionist and cubist artists, as well as that of Cezanne, Renoir, Braque and Matisse. The pigeons were stumped if Monet's paintings were turned upside down; while they could still identify an inverted Picasso.

Pierre Brassau was a mysterious avant-garde artist and the star of a show at Gallerie Christinae in Göteborg, Sweden, in February 1964, until his identity was revealed to be a chimpanzee at the local zoo as part of a hoax on modern art.

In the late eighteenth century Robert Barker (1739-1806) produced his 'monster panoramas', the largest paintings ever made at that time. These gargantuan, 360-degree hand-painted works spanned a canvas of 250sq. m to give the Georgian equivalent of a virtual-reality experience with tremendous city views, seascapes and battles. While touring a preview of a naval scene in London's Leicester Square in 1794, Queen Charlotte, wife of King George III, was made so seasick by the painting that she vomited into a lace handkerchief.

The origin of cinema can be found in these huge paintings. Entrepreneurs started producing 'moving panoramas', enormously long paintings that an operator slowly rolled before an audience like scenery passing by a train window. In America, the most famous of these were by John Banvard (1815-1891). His largest was the famous 'three-mile canvas', which was actually about 0.8km long. With the profits from touring his work he was able to build a giant imitation of Windsor Castle on Long Island, New York, which was nicknamed 'Banvard's Folly'.

In the silent film *Three Weeks* (1924) there's a scene in which Conrad Nagel lovingly scoops up Aileen Pringle and carries her to the bedroom. If you read her lips you'll notice that the actress seems to be telling her co-star, 'If you drop me you bastard I'll break your neck.'

There are two stars dedicated to Harrison Ford on the Hollywood Walk of Fame, commemorating different Harrison Fords. One is to the modern actor of *Indiana Jones* fame (b.1942), and the other to Harrison Ford (1884-1957), a silent film actor and Broadway star of the early twentieth century.

SOME BIRTH NAMES OF THE CELEBRATED

Joaquin 'Leaf' Bottom = Joaquin Phoenix

Archie Leach = Cary Grant

Marion Morrison = John Wayne

Caryn Johnson = Whoopi Goldberg

Ilyena Lydia Vasilievna Mironoff = Helen Mirren

Krishna Pandit Bhanji = Ben Kingsley

Edda Kathleen van Heemstra Hepburn-Ruston = Audrey Hepburn

Truman Streckfus Persons = Truman Capote

Howard Allen O'Brien = Anne Rice

Stevland Judkins = Stevie Wonder

Michael Boloton = Michael Bolton

No one knows how the Oscars got their nickname, although Bette Davies claimed it originated in her loud observation that the buttocks of the statue resembled those of her husband Harmon Oscar Nelson.

Irving Berlin is the only Academy Award presenter to announce their own name as the winner. In 1942 he won for Best Music in an Original Song for *White Christmas* and found the experience of awarding himself an Oscar so awkward that the rules of protocol were changed so it couldn't happen again.

Before George Clooney got his break on the TV show *E.R.*,
he was in a TV show called *E/R*.

When Anthony Hopkins called Quentin Tarantino's name as the winner
of Best Original Screenplay at the 1995 Academy Awards ceremony,
the television broadcast suddenly cut to black for two seconds. At the
time this was blamed on a technical glitch, but Tarantino's co-writer
Roger Avary later revealed that he had deliberately ruined the big
moment by bribing the cameraman tasked with filming a close-up of
Tarantino to turn his camera off. At the time the two were feuding
over Avary only being granted 'story by' credit, so that the film could
be stamped 'Written and directed by Quentin Tarantino'.[35]

35. Revenge can be served even subtler. In 2005, the literary critic A. N. Wilson
published an acclaimed biography of John Betjeman, which triumphantly featured
a previously unpublished love letter written by the poet that Wilson had been sent
by a woman named Eve de Harben. After Wilson's *Betjeman* was published, the true
provenance of the letter came to light. Years before, Wilson had written a scathing
review of Bevis Hillier's own 1988 biography of John Betjeman. In revenge, Hillier had
concocted the letter and sent it on to Wilson. The name Eve de Harben is an anagram
for 'Ever been had?', and the first letter of each line spells out 'A. N. Wilson is a shit.'*

*The practice of taking revenge through art is alive and well. In 2015 Daphne Todd,
the first female president of the Royal Society of Portrait Painters, admitted that
she had decided to take revenge on 'an obnoxious young gentleman' whose portrait
she had been commissioned to paint. She added devil horns to the picture, which
would become visible only after 50-100 years as the top layer of paint fades. 'I don't
think I did anything wrong on this particular portrait of this young gentleman,' she
told *The Independent*, 'as it didn't affect the final painting. What they have hanging
on their wall is a perfectly sensible painting.'

'WATCHING YOUR PERFORMANCE FROM THE LAST ROW.
WISH YOU WERE HERE.'
Telegram sent by George S. Kaufman to actor William Gaxton
during his production *Of Thee I Sing* (1933).

'NO MONEY TILL YOU LEARN TO SPELL.'
American film producer Carl Laemlle Sr, replying to a telegram
sent by his son that read: 'PLEASE WIRE MORE MONEY AM
TALKING TO FRENCH COUNT RE MOVIE.'

'OLD CARY GRANT FINE. HOW YOU?'
Cary Grant's response to a journalist's telegram asking
'HOW OLD CARY GRANT?'

During Muammar Gaddafi's (1942-2011) eccentric rule over Libya,
it was reported that a law was introduced prohibiting any Libyan but
him from playing as Colonel Mustard in the board game *Cluedo*. In
Arabic versions of the game, Colonel Mustard has the first turn.

There are many more possible moves in the ancient Chinese game of Go
than there are atoms in the observable universe. The number of atoms
is estimated at between 10^{78} and 10^{82}; the number of Go moves is 10^{170}.

The King of hearts was sometimes called the 'suicide king', as he
appears to be stabbing himself in the head with a sword. In fact, he's
holding an axe, but this detail has been lost over centuries of copying
by card makers.

Playing cards originated in China, most likely with the rise of woodblock printing during the Tang dynasty, around the ninth century AD. The first European playing cards appeared in the late fourteenth century, with suits of swords, staves, cups and coins. The four suits used today (spades, hearts, diamonds and clubs) were designed in France in the fifteenth century, and each figure in the pack is actually based on a specific historical and mythological hero/heroine:

King of spades = David (defeater of Goliath)

King of hearts = Charlemagne

King of diamonds = Julius Caesar

King of clubs = Alexander the Great

Queen of spades = Pallas/Athena

Queen of hearts = Judith

Queen of diamonds = Rachel

Queen of clubs = 'Argine', an anagram of Regina, thought to be Marie d'Anjou

Jack of spades = Ogier the Dane, a legendary paladin of Charlemagne

Jack of hearts = La Hire (a French military commander of the Hundred Years War)

Jack of diamonds = Hector of Troy

Jack of clubs = Judas Maccabee/Lancelot

The word 'trump' originates with *trionfi* ('triumphs'), a fifth suit of cards introduced to the Italian deck in the fifteenth century, which could beat any of the other four suits. This deck is the origin of the tarot card deck.

The word 'ace' comes, via Old French, from the Latin word *as*, meaning 'a unit', which was a small Roman coin. This was the nickname for the side of a die with only one mark. As it was the lowest score of the die, it came to also mean 'bad luck' in Middle English. When the ace became thought of as the highest playing card, its negative associations changed to those of excellence.[36]

In medieval chess, each pawn had its own profession. They were the Gambler (this and other lowlife professions were always placed on the 'sinister' left), the City Guard (placed before the left-side knight like the protective position taken by real city guards), the Innkeeper (in front of the left-side bishop), the Merchant (before the King), the Doctor (before the Queen), the Weaver (in front of their employer, the Bishop), the Blacksmith (in front of the right-side knight to tend to the horse) and the Farmhand (in front of the rook, as they were employed at the castle).

The Mechanical Turk was a chess-playing 'automaton' built in 1769 by Wolfgang von Kempelen (1734-1804) to impress Empress Maria Theresa of Austria. For eighty-four years the machine toured Europe

---

36. Speaking of aces, on 21 February 1929 the London *Times* reported that around eighty unemployed men in Middlesex, England, responded to a newspaper advertisement offering a week's paid work by a self-described 'flying ace with many distinctions'. They were to spend the week digging deep holes on a piece of land that happened to fall within the administration of two councils. The councils were soon notified about the excavations, but each authority assumed it was the project of the other, and so the men were left to dig in peace. The work continued for a week, and 'the flying ace' was well liked by the men. At the end of the week, however, he disappeared, and none of the men received any payment. Neither of the councils had authorised the work. The holes served no purpose.

and the Americas, trouncing human opponents in exhibition matches to the wonder of royal and imperial audiences. It survived to 1854, when it was destroyed in a museum fire in Philadelphia. Only then was it revealed by the son of its owner that the machine was an elaborate hoax, operated by an unidentified human chess-master hiding inside.

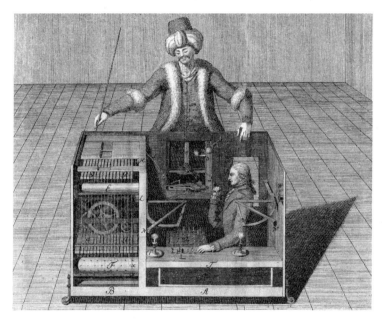

The Mechanical Turk, or Automaton Chess Player.

In 2022 a chess-playing robot in Moscow broke the finger of the seven-year-old boy it was playing against in an exhibition match. Witnesses said the boy made a fast move without waiting for the robot to finish its turn. 'A robot broke a child's finger – this is, of course, bad,' said Sergey Lazarev, president of the Moscow Chess Federation. 'The boy hurried, the robot grabbed him. We have nothing to do with the robot.'

Author J. M. Barrie (1860-1937) liked to terrorise children with prosthetics. Peter Llewelyn Davies, the inspiration for Barrie's hero Peter Pan, recalled being summoned to the writer's study while visiting with his family. He found Barrie sitting in the dimly lit room looking worriedly at the floor. When the young boy asked if something was the matter Barrie replied that there was something wrong with his feet. 'Glancing down,' said Davies, 'I saw to my horror that his feet were bare and swollen to four or five times their natural size. For several seconds I was deceived, and have never forgotten the terror that filled me, until I realised that the feet were artificial, made of the waxed linen masks, and that I had been most successfully hoaxed.'

A candidate for both left and right was found in 1967 when a foot powder was accidentally elected mayor of the Ecuadorian town of Picoazá. The confusion was down to a marketing stunt by the foot powder company Pulvapies, which ran an advertising campaign before the election with the slogan 'Vote for any candidate, but if you want well-being and hygiene, vote for Pulvapies.' They then went a step farther and circulated leaflets of the same size and colour as the official voting papers, titled 'For Mayor: Honorable Pulvapies'. The votes were counted, the foot powder won by a landslide. The losing candidates threatened to sue the pharmaceutical company that ran the ads, and the national election tribunal was instructed to untangle the mess.

The community of Rabbit Hash, Kentucky, has had a string of canine mayors since 1998, when a stray 'of unknown parentage' named Goofy Borneman-Calhoun was inaugurated in 1998 for a four-year term as a stunt to raise funds for the local historical society. His successor,

Junior Cochran, a black Labrador, enjoyed popularity with the voters but was controversially banned from the General Store on hygiene grounds. At the time of writing the position is held by a bulldog named Wilbur Beast, who thrashed Jack Rabbit the Beagle and Poppy the Golden Retriever in a landslide election victory in November 2020.

Before he was in office from 2010 to 2015, the fortieth president of Uruguay, José Alberto 'Pepe' Mujica Cordano, was a former revolutionary who spent fourteen years in captivity during the 1970s and 1980s, two years of which were spent alone at the bottom of a well.

Calvin Coolidge (1872-1933), US president from 1923 to 1929, loved to play pranks on his heavily armed Secret Service detail. On 21 January 1929, *Time* reported:

> In the wall of the north portion of the White House is a bell. On a recent afternoon, President Coolidge pressed this bell repeatedly, scampered quickly away. To the north portico rushed a detail of Secret Service men, to whom the bell's ringing was a summons to come at once. From a distance, the president watched their confusion … After the guards had dispersed, the president stole back, again pressed the button, again trotted away. Pleased, the president several times repeated his little prank. Eventually the Secret Service detail discovered the source of the false alarms, and put in another bell in a spot unknown to the president.[37]

---

37. 'The trouble with practical jokes is that very often they get elected.' – Will Rogers (1879-1935)

A set of 6m statues of the American presidents created by the artist David Adickes, which have languished in a field in Williamsburg, Virginia, since 2010, quietly disintegrating as they await a site suitable for their display to the public.

The English novelist J. L. Carr (1912-1994) liked to carve large stone heads in his garden, leave them to weather and then hide them in the grasses of old churchyards for future historians to have 'something to think about'.

The entire body of a starfish is actually its head. A 2023 study by researchers at the University of Southampton found that genes responsible for head development were found in every part of the young starfish, while the code for torso and tail sections were absent. It's thought they evolved to shed their body over time.

A stone, shell and obsidian hacha ('head') discovered at Veracruz, dating to AD 100-1000. Birth defects were thought of as blessings; Maya noblewomen would actively try to look cross-eyed, sometimes by wearing a dangling bead in front of their face.

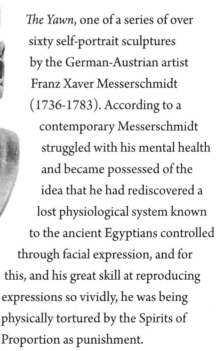

The Yawn, one of a series of over sixty self-portrait sculptures by the German-Austrian artist Franz Xaver Messerschmidt (1736-1783). According to a contemporary Messerschmidt struggled with his mental health and became possessed of the idea that he had rediscovered a lost physiological system known to the ancient Egyptians controlled through facial expression, and for this, and his great skill at reproducing expressions so vividly, he was being physically tortured by the Spirits of Proportion as punishment.

Tamrusiyah and her brother Mihrasb under the Waqwaq Tree. The mythical tree was said to grow screaming human heads as fruit. From a late sixteenth-century copy of *The Tales of Darab*, a medieval Persian prose romance.

Jill Drake, a classroom assistant in Tenderden, Kent, holds the record for the loudest scream at 129 decibels, which is slightly louder than the estimated volume of the Big Bang at 120 decibels. She set the record at a screaming competition held at London's Millennium Dome in 2000.

The loudest word ever shouted is 'quiet' – this Guinness World Record has been held by Irish primary schoolteacher Annalisa Wray since 1994, when she screamed the word at the Citybus Challenge in Belfast, Northern Ireland, at a level of 121.7 decibels.

The loudest noise ever heard by humans is believed to have been the eruption of Krakatoa, on 27 August 1883, at an estimated 310 decibels (acute pain is inflicted at 125 decibels, and irreversible ear damage can be caused at 140 decibels). Over 30,000 people were killed by the volcano and the ensuing tsunamis. The eardrums of sailors on a British ship 64km away called RMS *Norham Castle* were ruptured, and the blast was heard as far away as 4800km. The sound echoed around the world four times.

In 1957 the American military experimented with a 2.7m-long 'shouting bomb' that was designed to broadcast propaganda to those below as it drifted to the ground on a parachute. Deployed safely at 18,300m, parachutes opened and at 1200m a tape recorder began to loudly deliver a three-minute audio message, which tests showed could be heard across more than 1.3sq. km.

Though it's less than 5cm long, the 'snapping shrimp' or 'pistol shrimp' is one of the loudest creatures in the ocean – and it's only going to get louder as the oceans get warmer. The shrimp gets its name for the enormous claw it wields, which is about half the size of its body. It can snap this claw so quickly that it generates a bubble, which implodes at a volume louder than a gun firing a bullet. This stuns its prey, enabling it to attack. It's so loud that it's been known to interfere with sonar and whale song. As shrimps are cold-blooded, warmer water means their muscle activity increases, so with global warming it's likely we'll hear more of their pistol-popping sound on instrumentation in the future.

The Joan Sutherland Theatre in the Sydney Opera House has, unusually, a net above its orchestra pit. This was put in during the 1980s after a performance of the opera *Boris Godunov*, when a live chicken featured in the show wandered off the stage and fell onto a startled cellist.

The formidable, 1.9m, 150kg, basso Luigi Lablache (1794-1858) once performed in an opera as a prisoner languishing in a dungeon. When he sang the opening words 'I'm starving', the audience burst out laughing. A performance of *Rigoletto* in 1970 in Chile ended prematurely when the Canadian baritone Louis Quilico (1925-2000) leant his head back to take a deep breath, swallowed a pigeon feather that had drifted down from the rafters, choked and fainted.

The Nazi propaganda minister Joseph Goebbels (1897-1945) formed a big band with the idea of brainwashing the Allies with hypnotic swing music. Performances by Charlie and His Orchestra were broadcast from Germany with powerful transmitters to the USA, Canada and England, where listeners idly tuning their radios might have come across Nazi swing renditions of 'I Got Rhythm', 'Stardust' and 'The Sheik of Araby'. The songs began normally enough until about halfway through, when the band leader 'Charlie' (Karl Schwendler) would stop singing and launch into a Nazi propaganda speech. Sometimes this was sung to the music: 'Thanks for the memories/It gives us strength to fight/For freedom and for right/It might give you a headache, England/That the Germans know how to fight/And hurt you so much.'

In 2008 researchers at the Rowland Institute of Harvard University trained carp to tell the difference between baroque music and the blues of John Lee Hooker by pressing buttons with their snouts. Meanwhile, in Tokyo, Shigeru Watanabe at Keio University showed that Java sparrows can not only distinguish between Bach and Schoenberg but can also tell the difference between Vivaldi and the modernist works of Elliott Carter. Watanabe's sparrows preferred the more harmonious passages and sat in silence to enjoy them.

Stockhausen's *Helikopter-Streichquartett*, first performed in 1995, is a composition that requires four helicopters and a string quartet with strong stomachs. First the musicians are introduced, then they each board a separate helicopter with their instruments and together perform the piece in formation while circling the auditorium, keeping to a distance of 6km. The audience follow the aeronautic performance via audio and video monitors. The piece ends when the helicopters land and the musicians return to the stage to the sound of rotor blades winding down.

SOME MUSICAL UNAPPRECIATION

'Debussy's music is the dreariest kind of rubbish.
Does anybody for a moment doubt that Debussy
would write such chaotic, meaningless, cacophonous,
ungrammatical stuff, if he could invent a melody?'

New York Post, 1907

o

'It is probable that much, if not most, of
Stravinsky's music will enjoy brief existence.'

New York Sun, 16 January 1937

o

'Sure-fire rubbish.'

New York Herald Tribune on *Porgy and Bess*, 11 October 1935

o

'It will leave no great trace upon the history of our lyric theatre.'

Carlo Bersezio in *La Stampa*, on Puccini's *La Bohème*, 1896

o

'This music leaves an evil impression with its broken rhythms,
obscurity and vagueness of form, meaningless repetition
of the same short tricks ...'

Cesar Cui on Rachmaninov's Symphony No.1, 1897

o

'... Sounded as if a bomb had fallen into a large music factory
and had thrown all the notes into confusion.'

The Berlin Tribune on Wagner's *Tristan and Isolde*, 1871

'If the composer chances to come upon the path of a clear and
simple melody, he throws himself back into a wilderness of musical
chaos – in places becoming cacophony.'

1936 *Pravda* review of Shostakovich's *Lady Macbeth of Mtensk*

o

'But how did you get to understand Beethoven?'

wrote John Ruskin to John Brown in 1881. 'He always
sounds to me like the upsetting of bags of nails, with
here and there an also dropped hammer.'

o

'Tchaikovsky's First Piano Concerto, like the first pancake, is a flop.'

Nicolai Soloviev, *Novoye Vremya*, St Petersburg, 13 November 1875

o

'Tchaikovsky's Violin Concerto gives us for the first time the
hideous notion that there can be music that stinks to the ear.'

Critic Edvard Hanslick, 1881. Tchaikovsky memorised Hanslick's
review and would on occasion recite it word for the rest of his life.

o

Tchaikovsky's *1812 Overture* is 'very loud and noisy and completely
without artistic merit, obviously written without warmth or love,'

according to Tchaikovsky.

o

'Something that I literally can't bear listening to because
it absolutely reeks of cow-pies, exaggerated Norwegian
nationalism and trollish self-satisfaction!'

Edvard Grieg in an 1874 letter to a friend, about his own
composition, *In the Hall of the Mountain King.*

The German Jesuit scholar Athanasius Kircher (1601-1680) attempted to notate birdsong in his musical study/experimental compendium *Musurgia Universalis* (1650).

The story of the Pied Piper of Hamelin, in which a vengeful rat-catcher with a magical flute leads a town's children into a cave from which they're never seen again, appears to originate in an actual mysterious tragedy that struck Hamelin *c*.1284. The earliest written record of the event is in the town chronicles in an entry from 1384, which states: 'It is 100 years since our children left.' No one has been able to establish what this mournful note refers to.

The *Bal des Ardents* ('Ball of the Burning Men') was a masquerade ball held for Charles VI of France on 28 January 1393 in Paris that went disastrously wrong. Five French nobles were performing a dance dressed in costume as 'wild men' when they caught fire. The musicians kept playing as four of the men burnt to death, while the fifth survived by jumping into a vat of wine.

The Ball of the Burning Men, illustrated in a c.1470 copy of Jean Froissart's Chroniques.

In 1973 the English dancer Wayne Sleep became the first person to successfully perform an *entrechat-douze*, a ballet jump in which he crossed and uncrossed his straight legs at the calf five times in a leap lasting just 0.7 seconds. The record still stands today.[38]

Ballet remains banned in Turkmenistan, ever since former president Saparmyrat Niyazov (1940-2006) declared it, along with opera, as incompatible with Turkmenistan culture. Niyazov was just warming up. He also banned gold teeth; the circus; recorded music at weddings and public events; men from listening to car radios, growing beards or having long hair; and smoking in public places. He built a huge artificial lake and a gigantic cypress forest in the Kara Kum desert to change its climate; and renamed the months of the year after members of his own family.

Following Niyazov's death in 2006 his former personal dentist Gurbanguly Berdymukhammedov took power and permitted opera to be performed, but kept the ballet ban in place. Berdymukhammedov has his own quirks. Fond of the colour white, he banned the import of black cars, ordered every civil official to drive a white car, and ordered the citizens of the capital Ashgabat to have their cars repainted white or face heavy fines.

---

38. As impressive as this is, it somehow pales in comparison to another leg-based record, for the most kicks to one's own head made in a single minute: 147, achieved by Koki Takashima in Ichikawa, Chiba, Japan, on 27 April 2019.*

  *When you get other people to do the kicking, however, that's when things get felonious. In 2008 Jarrett Loft, twenty-eight, of Guelph, Ontario, was sentenced to sixty days in jail for approaching seven different women in the street and asking them to kick him in the groin. After they obliged, he thanked them and cycled away. Loft told the court that he had been 'acting out of curiosity'.

Dietrich Graf von Hülsen-Haeseler (1852-1908) was an infantry general of the German Empire and Chief of the German Imperial Military Cabinet who died of a heart attack while drunkenly dancing in a tutu for Kaiser Wilhelm II. On 14 November 1908, Von Hülsen-Haeseler was on a hunting trip in honour of the kaiser at Donaueschingen Castle in Donaueschingen, Baden. In the middle of a formal evening event, the heavyset moustachioed Von Hülsen-Haeseler entered unexpectedly dressed as a ballerina in a pink tutu and rose wreath. He began dancing for the kaiser and his guests, performing pirouettes, jumps, capers and blowing flirty kisses to the audience. He then bent over, apparently exhausted and fell to the floor dead. The circumstances of his death were covered up by the officer corps, who were keen not to add to the public furore over the ongoing public outrage over the 'Hülsen-Haeseler' affair, a gay scandal within the kaiser's circle that Von Hülsen-Haeseler had actually helped to cover up.

The North Korean dictator Kim Jong-il (1941-2011), born Yuri Irsenovich Kim, composed six operas and loved to stage musicals. He also had South Korean filmmakers Shin Sang-ok and Choi Eun-hee abducted and taken to North Korea in 1978 and ordered them to make movies for him. Before they escaped in 1986, they made a number of movies for the dictator, the last of which *Pulgasari* (1985), a Godzilla-knockoff about a dragon toy that comes to life, fights for the people and destroys the Emperor's palace.

SOME SELF-BESTOWED TITLES OF NORTH KOREA'S KIM JONG-IL

Eternal Bosom of Hot Love

Guardian Deity of the Planet

Dear Leader Who is a Perfect Incarnation of the Appearance
That a Leader Should Have

Master of the Computer Who Surprised the World

Man with Encyclopaedic Knowledge

Supreme Commander at the Forefront of the Struggle Against
Imperialism and the United States

Humankind's Greatest Musical Genius

Greatest Saint Who Rules with Extensive Magnanimity

Power Incarnate with Endless Creativity

Glorious General, Who Descended from Heaven

Present-day God[39]

---

39. Fath-Ali Shah Qajar (1769-1834), second shah (king) of Qajar Iran, was so proud
to have read the entire third edition of the *Encyclopædia Britannica* that he amended
his official title to include the honorific 'Most Formidable Lord and Master of the
Encyclopædia Britannica'.

According to his official biography, the first time Kim Jong-il picked up a golf club in 1994 he played a 38-under par round with eleven holes-in-one. At university, he wrote 1500 books in three years. He was said to be able to affect the weather with his moods and would order his female staff to inspect every grain of his rice to ensure it was the right length, weight and colour.

Genghis Khan (1162-1227) killed so many people that he cooled the planet. A 2020 study by Julia Pongratz of the Carnegie Institution's Department of Global Ecology found that, as a result of the 40 million people killed during the Mongol invasion of the thirteenth and fourteenth centuries headed by Khan, huge areas of cultivated land returned to forest. This absorbed an estimated 700 million tonnes of carbon from the atmosphere.

Adolph Hitler's (1889-1945) great-nephews live in Long Island, New York. Two are landscapers, one is a social worker. Their father, William Patrick Hitler ('my loathsome nephew' as Hitler called him) moved to America in 1939 and changed his surname. He fought in the US Navy in the Second World War and earned a Purple Heart. Joseph Stalin's (1878-1953) granddaughter is a Buddhist antiques dealer living in Oregon. Napoleon Bonaparte I's (1769-1821) great-great-great-great-nephew married the great-great-great-niece of Napoleon's second wife, Archduchess Marie-Louise of Austria. 'When I met Olympia,' said Jean-Christophe, Prince Napoléon, 'I plunged into her eyes and not into her family tree.'

The descendants of Aaron Burr (1758-1836) and Alexander Hamilton (1755/57-1804) go kayaking together. In contrast to their famous duelling forefathers, Hamilton Woods told the *New York Post* that he and his friend Antonio Burr 'find ourselves usually on the same side' of arguments.

On 3 May 1808 M. de Grandpré and M. de Pique settled a quarrel over the affections of a dancer named Mademoiselle Tirevit by duelling from the baskets of hot-air balloons 600m above Paris. De Pique fired first and missed; Grandpré scored a hit that collapsed de Pique's balloon and sent it crashing to the rooftops below, killing both him and his companion.

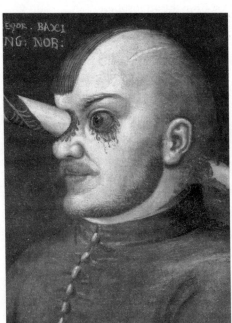

Sixteenth-century portrait of Hungarian nobleman Gregor Baci, who was impaled with a lance during a tournament. He lived for another year with the sawn-off piece lodged in his head.

A guide to the art of the husband vs wife duel as a way of resolving issues that can't be settled with words, as instructed in the 1459 fight-book of the German fencing master Hans Thalhoffer (*c*.1412-1482).

'The Guard of the Sword and Cloak oppos'd by the Sword & Lanthorn', from Domenico Angelo's *The School of Fencing* (1787). This is a guide to fighting a duel by dazzling your opponent with a lantern while thrusting your sword. The other figure demonstrates how to defend yourself with your cloak, which can absorb the thrust or be thrown over your opponent's head.

Employees of Brock's fireworks company, London, prepare to have a boxing match with their entire bodies wrapped in asbestos under a wicker framework of high-powered fireworks as part of a free show routinely held for the public from the late nineteenth century, called 'Living Fireworks'.

Jippensha Ikku was the pseudonym of the prolific Japanese writer and illustrator Shigeta Sadakazu (1765-1831), author of the twelve-part masterpiece *Tōkaidōchū Hizakurige,* and a habitual prankster. When he died on 12 September 1831, in the late Edo period, his body was laid on a traditional funeral pyre. Ikku's students honoured his last request and delicately placed next to his body several packages that he had prepared for the occasion while alive. His orders dutifully carried out, prayers were said and the pyre lit. And then all hell broke loose. As a final prank, Ikku had filled the packages with firecrackers.

The first automatic machine gun was devised by the inventor of hair-curling irons, mousetraps and steam pumps. Sir Hiram Maxim (1840-1916) also claimed to have invented the light bulb. In 1884 he demonstrated the new 'Maxim gun' to Queen Victoria, machine-gunning 'VR' (Victoria Regina) into a brick wall. By 1913 he was clearly missing target-shooting – he rented a room at the top of a high-street building in London and spent hours using a peashooter to fire black beans at a Salvation Army band that would play across the road.

An extraordinary fact about the estimated 8000 soldiers, 520 chariot horses and 150 cavalry of China's Terracotta Army is that no two faces are the same. The heads themselves were made with a mould but the Qin artisans were under imperial orders to craft the faces by hand, furnishing each figure with unique features and expressions to represent a unique personality. A cunning warrior is denoted by graceful eyebrow and eyes, while the eyes of a brave soldier are wide and staring. A large head with a wide face, bushy eyebrows and big eyes suggests a simple and honest soldier; and so on.

During the Second World War the British searched for solutions as to how to bomb German U-boats in the mid-Atlantic, where they were beyond the range of aircraft. Geoffrey Pyke (1894-1948) of the Combined Operations Headquarters (a department of the War Office set up with the sole task of harassing the Germans with raids) came up with an extraordinary idea – to build the largest naval vessel ever assembled, at 600m long, to serve as an aircraft carrier, made not of metal but of ice and wood. Steel and aluminium being in short supply at this time, the plan was to use pykrete, a composite of 14 per cent sawdust and 86 per cent ice. A prototype of 'Project Habakkuk' was made on Canada's Patricia Lake, but due to rising costs the plan was shelved.

US President Jimmy Carter (b.1924) once sent off his jacket to be dry-cleaned, only later realising that he'd left 'the biscuit' (the nickname for a laminated card with the codes to the country's nuclear arsenal) in one of its pockets. When US President Ronald Reagan (1911-2004) was shot in 1981, the hospital staff that cut off his clothing found 'the biscuit' in one of his suit pockets but, not knowing what it was, stuck it in his shoe on the floor where it was left unattended for hours.

Some 2476 nuclear bombs have been detonated around the world since 1945 – 520 of those explosions took place after 1993.

Since 1950 the USA has misplaced at least six nuclear weapons that have never been recovered.

In 1969 US President Richard Nixon (1913-1994) once got drunk and ordered a nuclear strike on North Korea. According to senior CIA specialist George Carver, when the North Koreans shot down a US Naval patrol aircraft on 15 April, 'Nixon became incensed and ordered a tactical nuclear strike ... The Joint Chiefs were alerted and asked to recommend targets, but Henry Kissinger got on the phone to them. They agreed not to do anything until Nixon sobered up in the morning.'

The torch of New York's Statue of Liberty has been closed to the public since 1916 after an attack by German spies. The event, known as the Black Tom explosion, took place on 30 July 1916, when the USA had not yet joined the First World War, but were supplying weapons to the Allies. In retaliation Germany sent saboteurs to destroy US production and supply lines, who loaded 99 tonnes of trinitrotoluene (TNT) onto a barge. At 2.08 a.m. the detonations occurred, destroying 2 million tonnes of war materials packed into railway carriages at the Black Tom railway yard near the statue. One of the largest non-nuclear explosions in history, the explosion broke windows in Times Square and was felt as far away as Philadelphia. Four people were killed, and $20 million worth of damage was done. The USA joined the First World War eight months later on 16 April 1917.

In the Second World War the British parachuted dogs behind German lines to help British soldiers detect mines and track enemy soldiers. Not all of the dogs were willing to leap from aircraft and bribes of raw meat sometimes had to be employed.

In Britain the Special Operations Executive (SOE) was secretly set up in 1940 to conduct espionage, sabotage[40] and reconnaissance in occupied Europe. They did this with a number of bizarre techniques and inventions, including bars of garlic-flavoured chocolate that SOE agents would eat so that their breath would help them blend in. Another trick was to leave a dead rat stuffed with explosives on the coal near an enemy's boiler, so that it would be thrown on the fire and trigger an explosion. They also hid explosives in fake plastic animal droppings, moulded from dung supplied by London Zoo: mule droppings were used to blow up cars in Italy; camel dung bombs were used in North Africa. Even industrial-strength itching powder was inserted into German underwear, sometimes to great effect – one U-boat was forced to abandon its mission because the sailors were convinced they'd contracted a virulent skin disease.

During the Second World War the Nazis made one secret landing in the USA: in October 1943 a German U-boat crew stealthily built Wetter-Funkgerät Land-26 (Weather Station Kurt), an automatic weather station, in northern Labrador, Newfoundland. The weather station was forgotten until it was rediscovered in 1977.

In England during the Second World War the Bishop of Chelmsford suggested that, to improve public morale, the wail of air-raid sirens warning of impending bombings could be replaced with a recording of a 'gay cock-a-doodledo' played half a dozen times instead.

---

40. The word *sabotage* comes from the *sabot* ('wooden shoes') worn by French industrial workers, who would hurl their footwear into the workings of machines to grind production to a halt during labour disputes.

Decoy overshoes in the shape of human feet, referred to as 'sneakers', that SOE agents wore over their boots when landing on beaches in the Pacific. The bare 'footprints' would trick the Japanese into thinking that only natives had been in the area.[41]

During the Second World War Jack Warner (1892-1978), president of Warner Bros, was worried that Japanese bombers would mistake his buildings for the nearby Lockheed aircraft factory, so he had a 6m arrow painted on his roof with an enormous sign that read 'LOCKHEED THATAWAY →'.[42]

41. Similar shoes were used by an American gentleman named Tony Signorini, who between 1948 and 1958 routinely walked the sandy beaches of Florida at night wearing enormous iron, three-toed penguin feet. Local legend sprang up of there being a prehistoric 4.5m penguin hiding in the area, and several sightings were reported over the decades.

42. A more drastic attempt to camouflage Northern Ireland's Parliament Buildings was made during the Second World War, when the Portland stone façade was painted with a mixture made from cow manure. The disguise did the trick but removing the 'paint' after the war took seven full years, as it had stained the stonework. It never regained its original white colour.

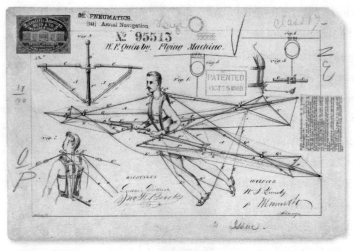

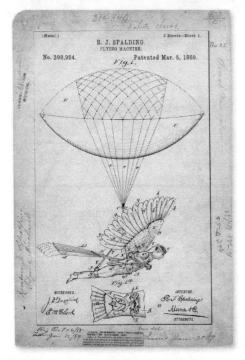

Above: Patent drawing for a flying machine invented by W. F. Quimby (1869).

Left: Patent drawing for R. J. Spalding's flying machine (1889).

Douglas Corrigan (1907-1995) was an American aviator and mechanic who earned the nickname 'Wrong Way' after he took off from New York, USA, for California on 18 July 1938, and mistakenly flew twenty-eight hours in the wrong direction across the Atlantic, landing at Baldonnel Aerodrome, County Dublin, Ireland. Corrigan claimed to have noticed his mistake only after

The front page of the New York Post *celebrating the return of the accidental navigator 'Wrong Way' Corrigan, 1938.*

twenty-six hours into the flight, blaming low visibility. He would never publicly admit to having made the crossing intentionally.

It was a precarious flight – the cockpit floor filled with leaking gasoline, his compass was twenty years old, his fuel tanks completely obscured his forward vision, he had no radio and his provisions were two chocolate bars, two boxes of fig bars and a bottle of water. The *New York Post* celebrated the heroic return of 'Wrong Way Corrigan' by printing their headline in reverse as tribute.

The first autopilot system was immediately used for the first instance of 'the mile-high club'. Lawrence Sperry (1892-1923), inventor of the first autopilot system, offered to take the married socialite Dorothy Peirce up in an autopilot-equipped Curtiss Flying Boat for a demonstration in November 1916. The plane crash-landed a short time later in water outside New York, USA. A pair of duck hunters rowed out to the crash site and found both Sperry and Peirce emerging from the wreckage completely naked. Sperry explained that the sheer force of the crash had stripped both he and Peirce of their clothing.

The 'jumping balloon' or 'hopper balloon' was a military invention in the 1920s that was immediately appropriated for a new sport, in which the bold and brainless strapped one to their backs and leapt into the air without any form of ballast or steering capability.

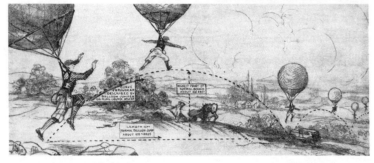

✱

The *America* was an airship built for Walter Wellman's 1910 attempt to cross the Atlantic Ocean by air, which departed on 15 October. At the last moment, a grey tabby cat named Kiddo was passed up to the radio operator on the ship to take along as a mascot. As it turned out, Kiddo didn't share the pioneering spirit and skittered around the ship in a mad panic, driving the six aeronauts to distraction. Not

Kiddo, the first cat to attempt a crossing of the Atlantic by airship, in the arms of Melvin Vaniman, the engineer of the airship America.

only was Kiddo the first cat to participate in an aerial crossing of the Atlantic, but the *America* was also the first air vessel to be fitted with a radio – and so the first ever radio transmission from an aircraft to the ground was: 'Roy, come and get this goddamn cat.'

Alberto Santos-Dumont (1873-1932), the Brazilian aeronaut and pioneering airship inventor, would throw 'aerial dinner parties' at his home, in which he had his guests sit on furniture suspended by wires from his high ceilings to experience the sensation of flight. The ceiling collapsed after one party, so instead he had new furniture made with legs so long that the diners had to climb a stepladder to take their seats.[43]

Jack Valentine Woolams (1917-1946) was an American test pilot who helped develop the Bell P-59 Airacomet, the first jet aircraft made in the USA, which was so secret that crew would attach a dummy wooden propeller to its nose when it taxied, to fool onlookers. Woolams liked to terrorise other pilots by dressing up as a gorilla in a bowler hat and smoking a cigar, and wave at them from his cockpit as he shot by.

Fufu (1997-2015) was a Thai Air Force officer and poodle, owned by Maha Vajiralongkorn, the crown Prince of Thailand. In 2007 US ambassador Ralph L. Boyce attended a gala dinner at the Grand Palace and was informed that Fufu had recently been promoted to Air Chief Marshal of the Royal Thai Air Force and was in attendance. Fufu appeared in full formal evening wear, including white gloves. Boyce reported that at one point the Air Chief Marshal would occasionally break protocol by leaping onto the dining table to drink from the guests' glasses.

---

43. Should sausages have been served at Santos-Dumont's dinner parties it would have been to the envy of German aeronauts, as during the First World War the production of sausages was temporarily banned across Germany so that the cow intestine skins could be repurposed for the production of zeppelins. Each airship required the guts of 250,000 cows to make the bags that held the hydrogen gas.

Only one dog has ever been officially enlisted in the United Kingdom's Royal Navy: Able Seaman Just Nuisance (1937-1944) was a Great Dane who served aboard HMS *Afrikander*. He did not have an exemplary record. Shortly after his commission as a morale booster in 1939, he was sentenced to seven days without bones for 'sleeping in an improper place', which the record notes was the petty officer's bed. He also fought with other mascots, and tended to sleep in corridors where servicemen would constantly trip over him. In 1944 he was buried at Simon's Town, South Africa, with full naval honours and a gun salute.

Laika is the famous Soviet street-dog-turned astronaut that was the first animal to orbit the Earth on board the Sputnik 2 spacecraft, which was launched on 3 November 1957. What's less well-known is that, ahead of the launch of the mission in which it was certain she would not survive, one of the scientists brought Laika home to play with his children to give her a pleasant experience. Dr Vladimir Yazdovsky wrote: 'Laika was quiet and charming … I wanted to do something nice for her: She had so little time left to live.'

An autographed headshot of Félicette, the first and only cat to be successfully sent to space. She was launched by the French Centre d'Enseignement et de Recherches de Médecine Aéronautique (CERMA) on 18 October 1963, and recovered alive after a thirteen-minute flight and a descent by parachute.

This print from Joan Blaeu's 1649 town book of maps of the Netherlands shows the test run of the enormous 'land yacht' or 'wind chariot' that took place *c*.1600. Built by the Flemish engineer Simon Stevin for the entertainment of his tutorial charge, Prince Maurice of Orange, the young Prince is shown at the helm, steering the colossal lumbering vehicle along a 22km stretch of beach between Scheveningen and Petten in just under two hours, an astounding pace that at times reached speeds exceeding that of horses. The accompanying inscription reveals that the young Prince enjoyed terrifying his passengers by pretending to lose control of it and driving straight towards the sea.

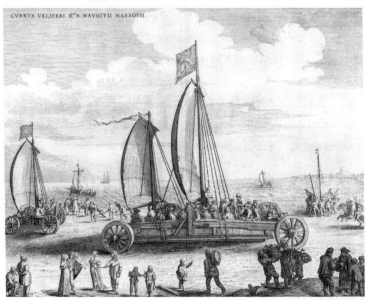

The earliest European mention of kites is made by Marco Polo (*c*.1254-1324), in a rare Latin translation of his thirteenth-century travels in China. And not just any kite; he describes seeing a man-carrying kite, launched for reconnaissance by a merchant ship as they embarked on a voyage: 'The men of the ship will have a wicker framework ... to each corner and side of that framework will be tied a cord, so that there are eight cords and all of these are tied at the other end to a long rope. Next they will find some fool or drunkard and lash him to the frame, since no one in his right mind or with his wits about him would expose himself to that peril.'

The 1921 Hélica propeller car, designed by French aeroplane engineer Marcel Leyat, which once clocked at an astonishing 170k/ph on the Montlhéry racetrack. The early models had no protective mesh in front of the giant blades – apparently the risk of colliding with, and shredding, stray pedestrians and pigeons was not a huge cause for concern. (Perhaps this is why *Popular Mechanics* once described it as 'an unsteerable murder machine.')

As a young man the Cambridge librarian Tim Munby repaired his 1925 Type-40 Bugatti roadster using pieces of vellum cut from a damaged manuscript. When people asked him about the age of the car, he enjoyed being able to say that 'parts of it date back to the fifteenth century'.

On 6 October 1909 a gentleman named Charles Cocking took Vancouver's first automobile ambulance out for a test drive, and immediately acquired Vancouver's first automobile ambulance patient, when he ran over Mr C. F. Keiss, an American tourist on his way to a hunting trip at Powell Lake.

Auto polo was a popular violent motorsport invented in 1911 in which players swapped polo ponies for Ford Model T motor cars. The high cost of repairing the colliding cars, and healing the broken bones of players, meant that its popularity waned in the late 1920s.

On 1 April 2001 the American restaurant chain Hooters told their employees that whoever made the most beer sales would win a free 'Toyota'. The winner, Jodee Berry, was ecstatic until receiving her prize: a toy Yoda doll, and a cheerful note from Hooters explaining that it had been an April Fool's joke. Jodee sued for breach of contract and fraud. After she won her case, her lawyer told reporters that the undisclosed settlement was enough to allow Jodee to 'pick out whatever type of Toyota she wants.'[44]

The first model trains were made for adults. Though they were initially created as engineering models, by the 1850s the miniatures were being marketed commercially as toys for adults not children. They didn't run on tracks either – instead these boiling-hot brass 'carpet railway' trains steamed their way across the living room floor on bare wheels, only stopping when the fuel ran out, when they collided with furniture or, as would often happen before safety valves were fitted, exploded. They left a snail-trail stain of boiling water and fuel on the carpet, leading to their nickname of 'Birmingham Dribblers'.

44. Incidentally The Toyota Motor Corporation was actually called 'Toyoda' (literally 'fertile rice paddies'), after its founder Sakichi Toyoda. It was changed in 1936 because the characters for Toyota only required eight brush strokes, a lucky number.*

*Sometimes a rebranding is more urgently required. Google, for example, was originally called BackRub.

The Dynasphere was the creation of physicist John Archibald Purves (1870-1952), who revealed his giant motorised monowheeled vehicle to the British public in 1932. The design of the Dynasphere was relatively simple: the driver's seat, controls and engine sat on rails, themselves inside a 3m, 450kg, circular cage of iron latticework. As this outer wheel revolved, the inner unit would (theoretically) remain level: a two-cylinder air-cooled Douglas engine of 6hp produced a top speed of 48km/h with a three-speed gearbox – there was even the option of reverse. Steering, though, was slightly trickier, requiring the driver to lean out into the direction he wished to turn. Deceleration was achieved simply by switching off the engine and gradually rolling to a halt. There were significant drawbacks to the design, the most significant of which was the high risk of 'gerbiling' – when the vehicle was accelerated or braked too sharply, the inner carriage and its driver would be spun around 360 degrees like a load of laundry on a heavy rinse cycle.

J. O. Lose's proposal for a one-wheeled velocipede with built-in umbrella, 1885.

In England in 2003, 2.5 million Mills & Boon romance novels were shredded and mixed into the foundation of a 26km stretch of England's M6 toll road to help bind the asphalt. An even stranger road component was employed in nineteenth-century Argentina, where a common way to repair potholes was to fill them with sheep heads.

Paris doesn't have a stop sign. Cars don't come to a full stop at any intersection that doesn't have a traffic light. Vehicles on the right have the right of way at both intersections and at roundabouts. There was one 'STOP' sign (literally 'STOP', which is considered a valid word in French borrowed from English) on the Quai Saint-Exupéry in Paris's sixteenth district, to which no one paid attention and which vanished sometime between 2012 and 2014 with no explanation.

The *Ponte delle Tette* ('Bridge of Tits') is a small bridge on the Rio di San Canciano in the parish of San Cassiano, Venice, Italy. It got its name from its historical popularity with prostitutes, who would stand topless atop it and in surrounding windows, using lanterns to illuminate their chests to drum up business.

One of the strangest street names in England is 'Whip-Ma-Whop-Ma-Gate', a short street in York running south from Colliergate to meet Pavement, Fossgate and the Stonebow. The name was first documented in 1505 as Whitnourwhatnourgate, and later as Whitney Whatneygate. It's thought that its meaning is 'neither-one-thing-nor-the-other street'.

In the mid-nineteenth century, the lack of citywide drainage in the American city of Chicago resulted in terrible epidemics of typhoid, dysentery and cholera. The engineer Ellis S. Chesbrough designed a plan in 1856 to install a citywide sewerage system, but there was one problem – many of the city's streets and buildings were at too low a level to facilitate natural drainage. The solution was simple: lift up the city. 'The Raising of Chicago' took place during the 1850s and 1860s, with engineers elevating central Chicago up out of low-lying swampy ground with standing water, physically boosting streets, pavements and entire buildings on jackscrews without causing any damage to the properties.

'A terrible place' is how the eighth-century charter of King Offa describes the medieval eyot of Thorney Island, where the British Houses of Parliament are now found.

On 31 January 2019 Hell froze over. Temperatures plummeted to a record low of -26°C, a depth of cold not experienced there for over a century. For the inhabitants of Hell, a small unincorporated community in Livingston County, Michigan (population about eighty or so; town slogan 'Go to Hell!'), the polar vortex that struck their homes was little more than an inconvenience, and not nearly as irritating as the national newspapers cackling over the irony.[45]

Volcán de Fuego ('Volcano of fire') is an active stratovolcano in Guatemala that has erupted every fifteen to twenty minutes since 1581.

---

45. There are two competing stories as to the origin of the naming of the town of Hell. The first is that on one dazzlingly sunny afternoon sometime in the 1830s a newly arrived German traveller stepped down from his stagecoach, squinted in the sunshine and remarked to his companion *So schön hell!* ('How beautifully bright!') This was overheard by a local, and the name stuck. To be honest I prefer the second explanation: the town's original settler, George Reeves, was asked for his thoughts on what the place should be called. Reeves reflected on the swarms of mosquitos, impenetrably thick forests, treacherous wetlands and other torturous local features and replied: 'I don't give a shit. You can name it Hell for all I care.' And lo, on 13 October 1841, the town of Hell was officially christened.

One of the greatest feats in twentieth-century urban engineering was successfully executed in Indiana, USA, in November 1930. In 1929 the Indiana Bell Telephone Company bought the Central Union building, and hired the architecture firm Vonnegut, Bohn & Mueller to work out how to demolish and redesign the building. Instead, the firm proposed something more imaginative: raise the seven-storey building up into the air on hydraulic jacks and rotate it ninety degrees for a better situation. Over thirty-four days the 11,000-ton building was rolled on 75-ton spruce beams at a speed of 40cm per hour, all without cutting off the phone lines of the call centre inside, which continued to operate, as well as maintaining the gas supply, water and electricity. The plan was masterminded by Kurt Vonnegut Sr (1854-1957), father of the novelist Kurt Vonnegut Jr (1922-2007).[46]

46. Interesting family, the Vonneguts. Kurt Vonnegut Jr's brother, Bernard (1914-1997), was an atmospheric scientist who discovered that silver iodide could be used in cloud seeding to induce rainfall. He also disproved an experiment by an Ohio professor named Elias Loomis, who in 1842 claimed (and bear with me here) that you could measure the speed of a tornado by firing a chicken out of a cannon, something he did repeatedly. Folk wisdom held that tornados left chickens stripped of their feathers, and so Loomis reasoned that finding the necessary velocity to effect this using a cannon would yield the k/ph windspeed of the weather phenomena. In 1975 Bernard Vonnegut proved this to be nonsense in a monograph entitled *Chicken Plucking as Measure of Tornado Wind Speed.*

The world's first seismology recording station, the Earthquake House, can be found in Scotland. Comrie village in Perthshire earned the nickname 'the Shaky Toon' from the thousands of small earthquakes that have rattled it since 1597, due to its position on the Highland Boundary Fault, where the highlands meet the lowlands.

In the entire US state of Wyoming there are just two escalators.

The US state of Alaska, located in the northwest corner of North America, is both the westernmost and the easternmost state in the USA – the Aleutian Islands, which belong to the state, extend into the Eastern Hemisphere.[47]

By a bizarre coincidence the geographical centre of North America is a town called Center. A geographer at University at Buffalo named Peter Rogerson read about the North Dakotan towns of Rugby and Robinson both claiming the title in 2015, basing their declarations on calculations made by the US Geological Survey in 1932. In 2016 he devised a computer program using an azimuthal equidistant map projection, and found that neither town was correct: instead, the centre of the USA was Center, North Dakota, which got its name from being at the centre of Oliver County.

The USA does not have an official language. Bolivia has thirty-seven official languages, the most of any country in the world.

---

47. Should you be in a contrarian mood you could always visit the city of Unalaska on Unalaska Island, Alaska.

The farthest part of North America is … in Australia? Sedimentary rocks in the rural Australian town of Georgetown, Queensland, were recently found to have signatures unknown in Australia, but strongly similar to sedimentary rocks in Canada. It's thought that 1.7 billion years ago the rocks were deposited in a shallow sea when the Georgetown area was part of the North American continent. It then snapped off from North America to collide with the Mount Isa region of northern Australia *c.*1.6 billion years ago, to form a supercontinent called Nuna. When this then broke apart, *c.*300 million years later, the Georgetown area became permanently stuck to Australia.

The only monarch in the world who speaks fluent Czech is the King of Cambodia. Norodom Sihamoni learned the language while he studied ballet in Prague for thirteen years.

The Spanish town of La Laguna, Tenerife, is the only place in the world where people speak backwards. A local barber named Francisco Fariña invented the 'Verres' language (*revés* is 'backwards', in Spanish) in the 1930s to confuse his customers. Today it's used widely by the elderly population. For example, *Nasbue chesno neragula, chesno de lohie y de ofri* is Verres for *Buenas noches lagunera, noches de hielo y frío* – 'Good evening people from La Laguna, nights of ice and cold.'

In 541, following the conquest of Antioch, Khosrow I, the Sassan Emperor and King of kings of Iran, built a new city near Ctesiphon (*c.*35km) southeast of present-day Baghdad to house the 30,000 or so Byzantine people he had captured. Bizarrely this new city was a duplicate of the original Antioch down to every last detail, and its citizenry were ordered to continue their lives exactly as they had lived previously in identical homes and workplaces. He called the new city Weh-Antiok-Xusrō, which literally means 'Better than Antioch, Khosrow Built This'.

There is a London Bridge in Lake Havasu City, Arizona, USA, that originally spanned the River Thames in London, England, from the 1830s. It was bought from the City of London in 1968 by an American entrepreneur called Robert P. McCulloch, who shipped it over and had it rebuilt in Arizona, brick by brick.

The city of Truth or Consequences in the US state of New Mexico was originally called Hot Springs but in 1951 renamed itself after the radio show *Truth or Consequences* to win a contest.

There is an Egyptian city called '6th of October' (*Setta Oktōbar*), in the Greater Cairo metropolitan area, with a population last recorded at 450,000. Established in 1979, the city was named in memory of the commencement of the 1973 Arab-Israeli War on 6 October 1973.

The US city of Portland, Oregon, had its name chosen in 1845 by tossing a penny. The alternative was Boston, Oregon.

The US city of Des Moines, Iowa, gets its name from *mooyiinkweena,* which is how the neighbouring Peoria tribe would refer to it and their hated neighbours who lived there. It literally means 'shit-faces'.

Spreuerhofstrasse Spalt in Reutlingen, Germany, is the world's narrowest street. It's 31cm wide. The 'street' has entered local slang in the context of dieting, as in: 'I'll know I've hit my target weight when I can fit through the Spreuerhofstrasse Spalt.'

The 'world's littlest skyscraper' can be found in Wichita Falls, Texas, USA. The four-storey building was built by J. D. McMahon, an engineer who conned the town into donating $200,000 (more than $3.3 million today) to construct a magnificent skyscraper that would put the city on the map. However, no one noticed that in the building contracts McMahon was quietly proposing a structure [12m] 480 *inches* tall, not [146m] 480 *feet* as he had boasted verbally. A lawsuit was brought, but the contract was found legally binding.

Forget Pisa – the Leaning Tower of Suurhusen, Germany, leans at an angle of 5.19°, which is 1.22° more than the 3.97° angle of the Pisa tower today. The German tower was built in the Middle Ages on a foundation of oak tree trunks, which gradually rotted away.

In 2013 Bland Shire in New South Wales, Australia, joined with the town of Boring, Oregon, USA and the village of Dull, Scotland, to form the League of Extraordinary Communities. Bland Shire council erected a sign saying 'Bland … far from Dull and Boring.'

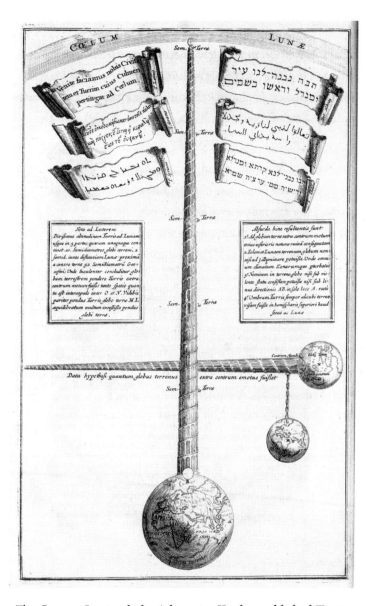

The German Jesuit scholar Athanasius Kircher published *Turris Babel* in 1679, demonstrating how impossibly high the Tower of Babel would have to be to touch Heaven.

There's a 129.50sq. km area in the Yellowstone National Park in which, as a result of a loophole in the Constitution of the United States, a person could theoretically commit any major crime including murder and avoid conviction. It's known as the Zone of Death.

In 1919 at Tall Al'Ubaid in Iraq, archaeologists uncovered several 7000-year-old lizard-headed figurines. The example shown here appears to be a lizard-woman suckling an infant. Created by the prehistoric Mesopotamian Ubaid culture, we don't know what the figurines represent.

Jouhatsu is the name given in Japan to the phenomenon of people deliberately vanishing and leaving no trace. This occurs around the world but it is particularly prevalent in Japan, where one estimation is that *c.*100,000 Japanese disappear annually, although because the subject is taboo this figure might be even higher when taking into consideration unreported disappearances. There is no database of missing persons in Japan.

The *Albero della Fecondità* ('Fertility Tree') is an extraordinary Italian fresco known locally as the 'penis tree'. Created in 1265 it was discovered only in 1999 in the street-level loggia ('balcony') of a thirteenth-century former wheat store in the town of Massa Marittima. It's thought the images of women collecting the tree's phallic fruit are related to the folklore of witches stealing men's genitals.

The barnacle goose tree, from Topographia Hibernica *(c.1188).*

To medieval authors the seasonal disappearance of birds, and their breeding process, were mysteries explained with the idea that they literally grew on trees. The Swedish writer Olaus Magnus (1490-1557) reported that a 'Scotch Historian, who diligently sets down the secret of things, saith that in the Orcades [Orkney Isles] Ducks breed of a certain Fruit falling into the Sea; and these shortly after get wings, and fly to the tame or wild Ducks.'

The largest seed in the plant kingdom is that of the *Lodoicea* tree, commonly known as the coco de mer. Weighing in on average at 15-30kg, it bears a striking resemblance to the disembodied buttocks of a woman on the front, and a woman's belly and thighs on the reverse. Hence its botanical name *Lodoicea callipyge*, from the Greek meaning 'beautiful buttocks'. The rare species of palm tree can be found in the Seychelles archipelago in the Indian Ocean, from where the giant nuts occasionally drift via ocean currents to other distant shores like those of the Maldives. Local legend said that on stormy nights the male trees would tear themselves from the ground, strut towards the females and have wild physical sex, producing more of their erotically shaped fruit. The fact that no one had ever actually *witnessed* this arbori-coitus was explained by the fact that the trees were shy and could steal the sight of any voyeur. The legend of the sex nuts continued into the Victorian era, when respected British Army officer and Christian cosmologist Major-General Charles George Gordon (1833-1885) declared the Seychelles to be the original location of the Biblical Garden of Eden, and that the coco de mer nuts were the forbidden fruit that Adam had bitten into and handed to Eve.

Most edible figs have a dead wasp inside. As part of the pollination process a fig is created when a small female wasp of the Agaonidae family crawls inside the syconium, a fleshy receptacle that will become the fig, and passes through the ostiole ('tunnel') lined with downward-facing scales that strip her of her wings and antenna, and prevent the wasp from leaving. If there are male flower parts it means she finds herself in what will be a caprifig, and after providing pollen, she lays her eggs. If she is surrounded by female flower parts then she is unable to store her eggs and is trapped, eventually dying inside what will be an edible fig. When you bite into a fig you won't be able to detect her carcass because enzymes called ficains break down the mother wasp carcass and turn it into protein that is absorbed by the fruit. And so the chances are high that every time you eat a fig you consume wasp biomass.[48]

---

48. One type of wasp, *Megaphragma mymaripenne*, would likely have little problem escaping this fig prison, given its size of just 0.2mm, making it the third smallest insect in existence – smaller, even, than a single-celled amoeba.

There is a tree in New York, USA, (shown here) that produces forty different types of stone fruit simultaneously. The 'Tree of 40 Fruit' was created by Professor Sam Van Aken at Syracuse University, who in 2008 began grafting branches from forty different donor trees onto one stock tree. Every year the tree produces its startling variety of fruit, including almonds, apricots, cherries, nectarines, peaches and plums, with a multicoloured blossom of red, pink and white leaves. At last count Van Aken has created sixteen different 'Trees of 40 Fruits'.

The term 'vegetarian' was introduced in 1842 – before that, vegetarians were called 'Pythagoreans', as vegetable diets were linked to the Greek philosopher Pythagoras (c.570-500/490BC). He reportedly avoided eating meat as he believed in metempsychosis, the transmigration of souls from humans to animals.

Pythagoras recoiling in horror from some beans in a c.1512 illustration.

Of all the legends involving Pythagoras, perhaps the strangest is his unwavering aversion to beans. Supposedly the philosopher forbade his followers from eating the vegetable for fear that the resultant passing of gas was the loss of a piece of one's soul. Unfortunately, one night Pythagoras was attacked by an angry mob and chased until reaching a bean field, which he couldn't bring himself to enter. Trapped, his pursuers fell on him with daggers.

A freshly sealed Egyptian tomb would probably have smelled quite strongly of onion. The vegetable in ancient Egypt was worshipped as a symbol of eternal life, due to its circle-within-a-circle structure. Mummified corpses have been found to have flowering onions stuffed into their chests, pressed into their pelvises and against their ears, attached to the feet and placed over the eyes (as was the case with the remains of King Ramses IV, who died in 1150 BC). Ancient Egyptian priests are shown holding onions in illustrations but were forbidden from eating them because it was believed eating onions greatly increased your sex drive.

Before it was known as 'The Big Apple', New York's
nineteenth-century nickname was 'The Big Onion',
as there were so many layers to explore.

Bibliophagia ('book-eating') occurs twice in the Bible. In Ezekiel 3:1-3, the prophet of exile is told by a heavenly voice to open his mouth and eat a scroll, and in Revelations 10:8-11, an angel delivers a similar meal to the author. Metaphorical examples aside, incidents of real bibliophagia are scattered throughout history. In 1373 a furious Bernabò Visconti forced two papal delegates to eat the bull of excommunication they had delivered to him, including its silken cord and lead seal. After satirising Bernhard, Duke of Saxe-Weimar, the Austrian politician Isaak Volmar (1582-1662) was made to swallow the pamphlets whole; while the seventeenth-century German lawyer Philipp Andreas Oldenburger was sentenced to not only eat his writings that had so offended the authorities, but also to be flogged while doing so, until he had consumed every last page.

Uncooked red kidney beans are poisonous, as they contain the toxin phytohemagglutinin. Eating just five can cause vomiting and diarrhoea.

Physiggoomai – An ancient Greek term for a person excited by garlic.

The oldest archaeological evidence for soup is a 6000-year-old African recipe for a hippopotamus broth, prepared with hippo and sparrow meat, lentils and spices.

Koala bears make their own 'soup' – koala joeys feed on their mother's pap, a soupy nourishment that is formed in the mother's cecum ('intestinal pouch') before it's excreted. The cocktail of microorganisms in the koala soup helps prepare the joey's digestive tract for its diet of toxic leaves.[49]

The can-opener was invented fifty years after the can. Before the arrival of the 'can opening blade', which was essentially a saw that left a jagged rim, cans of food were opened with hammer and chisel. This was the manufacturers' recommended method, as the first cans were made of wrought iron, lined with tin and could be as thick as 3.5mm. Soldiers often used bayonets to pry open their food tins, and if that failed they shot them.

---

49. A similarly extraordinary animal substance is the soupy pupal matter that a caterpillar breaks down into during metamorphosis, where various body parts are liquified, before it is reconstituted into a butterfly. In 2008 it was discovered by researchers at Georgetown University that despite this obliterative process, butterflies somehow retain memories made during their caterpillar form.

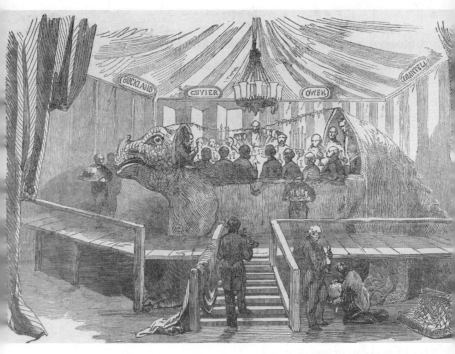

The sketch from The Illustrated London News *of the dinner inside the Iguanodon at the Crystal Palace, 1853.*

On New Year's Eve 1853, one of the strangest dinner parties in history was held inside a giant model of an iguanodon dinosaur. Benjamin Waterhouse Hawkins (1807-1894) invited a group of scientists, businessmen and newspapermen to dine inside the 9m-long dinosaur to help celebrate his creation of a series of dinosaur sculptures at the Crystal Palace. The guests were served seven lavish courses, of mock turtle soup, mutton cutlets, partridge stew, curried rabbit and fillets of sole with mayonnaise; followed by French pastries, jellies, puddings, fresh fruit and nuts for dessert. Hawkins's dinosaur models still stand today in the grounds of the Palace and are protected with the classification as Grade I listed buildings.

Humans are not at the top of the food chain – in fact we're in the middle, and 'cannot be considered apex predators'. This was established in 2013 by a team of French researchers who attempted to calculate the Human Trophic Level (HTL) and to position humans in the context of the food web. The metric is based on a species diet: primary producers such as plants and phytoplankton, for example, are trophic level one, whereas carnivorous apex predators like polar bears or killer whales are as high as 5.5. Humans, with their mixed diet of meat, fruits and vegetables, were positioned at a 2.5 – we're on a par with pigs and anchovies.

The first teabag was invented by two American women named Roberta C. Lawson and Mary Molaren, in 1901, c.2900 years after recorded tea drinking began. In 1908, a tea merchant named Thomas Sullivan popularised the teabag – accidentally. His tea leaves were supplied in silk drawstring pouches, meant to be emptied into the teapot. His customers assumed they were supposed to dip the bag into the water.

The Hawaiian pizza was invented in Canada by a Greek man. The California roll also originated in Canada. (And incidentally the Panama hat was created in Ecuador.)

Tomato sauce was a relatively late addition to Italian cuisine, as tomatoes were only introduced to Italy from the Americas in the sixteenth century.

The US Agricultural Research Service in Beltsville, Maryland, USA, came up with a new way of tenderising meat in 2000 that was remarkably efficient though slightly impractical as it involved high explosives. Rather than tenderise with a hammer, the researchers detonated the equivalent of a quarter-stick of dynamite with the meat in a rubbish bin filled with water. Not only did the shockwaves soften the meat, but they also found that their process killed food-poisoning bacteria like *E. coli*. Unfortunately, the rubbish bin was blown to pieces each time, and a larger container didn't work as well.

The Meat-Shaped Stone is the most celebrated treasure in the collection of Taiwan's National Palace Museum. The piece of jasper was carved to resemble a slab of Djongo pork belly marinated in soy sauce, made sometime in the Qing dynasty (1644-1912).

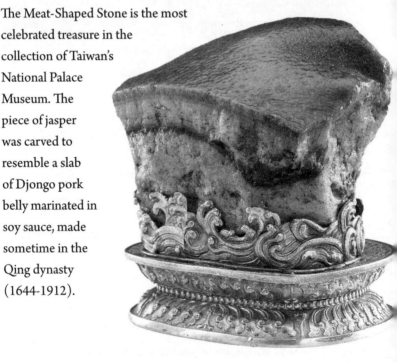

The US military created an indestructible sandwich in 2002 that would maintain sandwich integrity through airdrops, rough handling and extreme climates, and would stay 'fresh' for three years at 26°C about the temperature of a warm summer's day, or for six months at 38°C. The trick was minimising the amount of water in the ingredients, using fillings like pepperoni and chicken with humectants, which minimise moisture and thereby bacterial growth. The sandwiches were then sealed in airtight packaging. Soldiers apparently found them 'acceptable'.[50]

In 2012 Land Rover printed a guide for its Dubai customers to surviving the desert in the event of a mechanical breakdown. The pamphlet gives illustrated instructions on how to build shelters, signal for help, light a fire and hunt local wildlife, and how to get your orientation by using the north star. The metal binding can be removed for use as a cooking skewer, and the reflective packaging can help signal for help. As a last resort, the book urges you, eat it: the pages of the *Land Rover Edible Survival Guide* are made out of consumable paper and ink – the book claims to offer the same nutritional value as a cheeseburger.

---

50. In terms of preservation techniques, it seems we will all be aspiring to taste the next big thing in wine, 'undersea champagne'. In 2010 divers exploring Finland's Åland archipelago discovered a shipwreck from 1852 50m below the surface, with 145 bottles of champagne in its hold. The wine was recently tasted, and found to have aged to an unprecedented quality. Philippe Jeandet, a professor of food biochemistry at the University of Reims, was permitted to taste one droplet squirted from a microsyringe: 'I have never tasted such a wine in my life,' he declared. 'The aroma stayed in my mouth for three or four hours after tasting it.' A single bottle has been valued at $190,000. Veuve Clicquot immediately sank dozens more bottles at the exact spot, to be collected in forty years' time.

After Colonel Sanders (1890-1980) sold his company Kentucky Fried Chicken (KFC) in 1964, he made a hobby of visiting KFC restaurants unannounced to inspect the food. Anything substandard would loudly be deemed 'God-damned slop' and tipped onto the floor. In 1975 he was unsuccessfully sued by KFC's new owner for slander after he publicly grumbled that their gravy was 'sludge' with the flavour of wallpaper.

'Hints To Diners-Out', from Horace Raisson's *Code Gourmand* (1827): 'When you are seated next to a lady, you should be only polite during the first course; you may be gallant in the second; but you must not be tender till the dessert. When you have the misfortune to sit next to a child, your only plan is to make him drunk as soon as possible, that his mother may be forced to take him away.'

'Thank you madam, the agony is abated' – Lord Macaulay (1800-1859), aged four, after having hot coffee spilt over his legs.

Compared to drinking, alcohol intoxication begins much sooner if consumed rectally as it's absorbed directly into the bloodstream. The Maya people knew this, as they would ritually perform alcohol enemas, sometimes mixed with psychotropic drugs, via syringes made of clay to achieve a state of ecstasy.

In a 2012 study the residents of Vatican City were found to drink more wine per person than any other country in the world, at 74 litres per person annually. This is twice the French average and triple the British average.

Zhou, ruler of the Shang dynasty in China *c*.1075-1046BC, was said to have lost his empire due to his extreme debauchery. Notably he built an enormous lake, filled it with wine, then ordered naked men and women to chase each other around in it.

When we think of paint-hurling artists like Jackson Pollock (1912-1956) we should also add Chinese artist Wang Hsia (*fl.*785-805), whose work sadly has not survived. Known as Ink-flinger Wang, the *Register of Notable Painters of the T'ang Dynasty* of 840 recounts how Wang loved to get drunk and work by throwing ink on silk at random, smearing it with his hands, his feet and his backside, and then produce shapes of mountains and rivers out of the chaos. 'When he was drunk, he would spatter ink on it, laughing and singing all the while. He would kick it, smear it with his hands, sweep his brush about or scrub with it.' (The writer Chang Yen-yuan (*fl.*847) mentions that Ink-flinger Wang also enjoyed drunkenly dipping the topknot of his hair in the ink, and then head-butting the fabric.)

In 2015 Scotland produced its first wine. The Savoy-trained chef Christopher Trotter planted a vineyard in Fife in 2012 and three years later the first vintage of the dry white Chateau Largo appeared. Critics hailed it as 'undrinkable'. Chef Trotter himself described it as 'not great'. Richard Meadows of the Great Grog wine merchant in Edinburgh told *The Sunday Times*: 'It's not yet drinkable but, that said, I enjoyed it in a bizarre, masochistic way.'

🍽

When short on vitamin supplements you always have the option of drinking rainwater, which can contain vitamin B12; or tears, which have been found to contain vitamin A. Additionally, the needles of some pine trees are rich in vitamins A and C.

🍽

Iceland imports its ice. On average it's 40 per cent cheaper for its supermarkets to source ice from countries like Norway, the UK and the USA than it is to buy Icelandic ice.

🍽

In 2012 it was discovered that injecting humans with a substance found in the saliva of the Gila monster, North America's only venomous lizard, can halt cravings for sweet and savoury snacks and alcohol.

🍽

20 Slices of American Cheese (2018) by the New York publisher Ben Denzer is a book literally made of cheese. Its bright yellow clothboard binding holds twenty individually wrapped American single cheese slices. A box of twenty-four slices of Kraft American cheese slices costs $3.50 roughly – the ten copies of *20 Slices . . .* sold for $200 each.[51]

🍽

Before people said 'cheese' while having their picture taken, in the nineteenth century they said 'prunes'. The earliest mentions of photographers instructing subjects to 'say cheese' are found in newspapers of the early 1940s.

---

51. Denzer's other works, by the way, include *200 Fortunes*, a small volume of Chinese restaurant fortunes; *$200 in Order*, a book of 200 one-dollar bills; the even more self-explanatory *30 Napkins from the Plaza Hotel*; and *20 Sweeteners*, an elegantly bound collection of twenty artificial sweetener packets.

Since 1953 the regional bank Credito Emiliano in northern Italy has accepted wheels of Parmigiano-Reggiano cheese as collateral for small-business loans. The service is primarily used by local dairy farmers who face long lead times and need to save on operating costs. The cheese is stored in climate-controlled vaults.

Until 2004 a French cheese called Époisses de Bourgogne was regularly voted the foulest-smelling cheese in the world. Aged for an average of six weeks in brine and brandy, its aroma is so noxious that it's reportedly banned on French public transport. In 2007 researchers at Cranfield University, England, used an 'electronic nose' sensor to test fifteen different cheeses and declared the cheese Vieux Boulogne to be the stinkiest, attributed to its beer-brushed rind reacting with the dairy. A *Daily Telegraph* reporter agreed, describing Vieux Boulogne's odour as being reminiscent of 'unwashed feet and unwashed tom cat'.

On 12 June 1885 *The New York Times* reported that an Irishwoman named Teresa Ludwig was prevented by a police officer from jumping into the Hudson River. When asked why she had attempted to do so, she responded that 'death was preferable to the constant fumes of Limburger cheese' favoured by her German husband.

Phrynarachne ceylonica, otherwise known as the Asian bird-dung crab spider, is known for its horrible, dunglike odour that it discharges to attract prey and deter predators. If a predator approaches despite the smell, the spider curls up to convincingly resemble bird faeces.

The African elephant has a superb nose, probably superior across the animal kingdom, allowing it to detect water sources up to 19km away. Of all animals it's been found to have the most scent receptors and genes associated with smell – five times as many as humans, and more than twice those of dogs. Researchers in Angola found that elephants were avoiding minefields because they could smell TNT. A Japanese study from 2015 also found that elephants in Kenya used scent clues to distinguish between the Maasai tribe, who traditionally spear them and whom they avoid, and the Kamba, who aren't a threat.[52]

The Osmothèque is a fascinating archive located in Versailles, France, devoted entirely to preserving historical and present perfumes. It was first proposed to the Société Française des Parfumeurs in 1976, and since its founding it has accumulated well over 3000 perfumes kept in a controlled environment by the institute's 'osmocurators'. Some of the rarest historical scents and ancient perfumes – like the Parfum Royal of the Parthian kings, mentioned by Pliny the Elder in the first century – sit alongside medieval eau de toilettes like: the Eau de la reine de Hongrie of Elizabeth of Poland from the fourteenth century; the eighteenth-century Poudre de Chypre; and an eau de cologne made by Napoleon's manservant Louis-Etienne Saint-Denis, also known as Mameluke Ali, in 1815 during his exile on Saint Helena.

| 52. Incidentally, no one has ever seen an elephant jump.

Calvin Klein's cologne Obsession for Men has been used by zookeepers around the world, and forest rangers in central India, to pacify tigers. The scent contains civetone, a pheromone secreted in the perineal gland of the civet, a small carnivorous mammal. When big cats like tigers catch a scent of civetone they try and bask in it. Wildlife photographers and conservationists sometimes use civetone-rich cologne to lure cats to the camera lens.

In addition to manufacturing Biro pens, the company BIC has also dabbled in producing fragrances. These include BIC Homme, BIC Sport, BIC Day For Women, BIC Night For Women, the DOT collection and BIC Nuit (which really seems too close to 'Biscuit' – but what do I know). These were discontinued a while ago, but according to the company are still available to buy in Iran.

The port city of Tacoma, Washington, USA, has been haunted by an overpoweringly noxious odour of rotten eggs since at least the early twentieth century, which has been blamed on various local factors including the local paper mill, rendering plant and oil refinery. Things weren't helped in 1997 when, at the height of a humid summer, city workers opened up a giant sewage tank that had been sealed for fifteen years. Over the years the mystery smell has been reduced, but somehow still lingers. It's known as the Aroma of Tacoma.

John Aubrey, writing in *Brief Lives* (1693), noted: 'This Earle of Oxford [Edward de Vere, 17th Earl, 1550-1604] making his low obeisance to Queen Elizabeth, happened to let a Fart, at which he was so abashed and ashamed that he went to Travell, 7 yeares. On his returne, the Queen welcomed him home, and sayd, "My Lord, I had forgot the fart."'

Also on the subject of noble gasses, on 23 March 1853 Karl Marx (1818-1883) wrote to Friedrich Engels (1820-1895) about the Empress Eugénie, consort of Napoleon III (1826-1920):

> That angel suffers, it seems, from a most indelicate complaint. She is passionately addicted to *farting* and is incapable, even in company, of suppressing it. At one time she resorted to horse-riding as a remedy. But this having now been forbidden by her Bonaparte, she 'vents' herself. It's only a noise, a little murmur, a nothing, but then you know that the French are sensitive to the slightest puff of wind.

In response to a call by the Royal Academy of Brussels for scientific papers, Benjamin Franklin (1706-1790) once wrote an essay called 'A Letter to a Royal Academy About Farting', or 'Fart Proudly', *c.*1781, in which he suggests scientists should develop a drug that could be mixed with food and sauces to render the odour of flatulence as 'agreeable as Perfumes'.

The word partridge means 'farter' – the etymology of the name for the four-toed Eurasian bird can be traced back via Old French and Latin to the Greek name for the bird, *perdix*. This was derived from *perdesthai*, 'to fart', referring to the whirring noise of the bird's wings in flight.

He-Gassen (literally: 'Fart competitions') in a Japanese scroll of the
Edo period (1603-1867) by an unknown artist, depicting characters
exercising flatulence against each other, likely as satire.

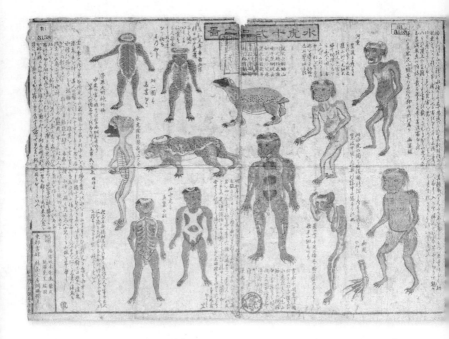

Suiko juni-hin no zu ('Illustrated Guide to 12 Types of Kappa')
of mid-nineteenth century Japan, warning of a water spirit
that was known to haunt outhouses.

American inventor Joseph C. Gayety (1827-1895) devised the first
commercial toilet-paper roll in 1857, although it can't have been the
most comfortable experience as it wasn't until 1935 that a 'splinter-
free' toilet paper was invented by the Northern Tissue Company.

Yugoslav politician Milovan Đilas (1911-1995) was imprisoned for
ten years for his anti-communist criticism of Josip Broz Tito's (1892-
1980) presidency. While behind bars he translated John Milton's
Paradise Lost into the Serbo-Croat language, writing out the entire
work on toilet paper.

The Danish Arctic explorer Peter Freuchen (1886-1957) was trapped by a blizzard during an expedition in 1926 and buried under snow and ice. Having no tools to hand, he claimed to have used one of his frozen faeces as a chisel and dug his way out. He then crawled for three hours back to base, where he amputated his own toes.

The Italian artist Piero Manzoni (1933-1963) produced *Merda d'artista* ('Artist's Shit') in 1961. In this series of sealed, 30g cans, limited to a set of ninety, each one carries a label written in Italian, English, French and German that claims the contents of the can to be Manzoni's own excrement: 'Artist's Shit. Contents 30 gr net. Freshly preserved. Produced and tinned in May 1961.' In October 2015 *Tin 54* sold at Christie's for £182,500; then in August 2016 at an art auction in Milan another tin sold for €275,000. The cans are steel and therefore can't be X-rayed, and no one has dared open a tin to check, as this would severely reduce its value.[53]

53. Manzoni had some fabulously imaginative and wry proto-conceptual ideas. *Magisk Sockkel* ('Magic Bases', 1961) is a set of wooden plinths that, when stood on by the viewer, transforms their status to 'Living Sculptures'. Similarly, *Socle du Monde* ('Base of the World', 1961) is a large plinth inscribed with 'The Base of The World, Homage to Galileo', which was placed upside down in a field in Herning, Denmark, turning the entire world into an inverted work of art. *Linee dalla lunghezza eccezionale* ('Lines of Exceptional Length', 1960-1961) comprised lines drawn on rolls of paper using a rotary press and a large dripping bottle of ink – the longest of these lines ran for 7.2km. The plan was for a *Linee* to be produced for each major city in the world, where it would be kept in a steel tube. If all were to be unrolled and joined together, the total length of the *Linee* would equal the length of the equator and circle the world. (Sadly, Manzoni died before this project was finished.)

According to a YouGov survey published 16 May 2023, the majority of German men sit down to pee. British and American men are among the least likely to do so. This despite the fact that in Germany there is the mocking term *sitzpinkler* for someone who sits down to pee. (People who urinate in the street are called *Wildpinkler*.) Urologistically speaking, sitting helps you empty your bladder more efficiently, especially for men with enlarged prostates, and helps prevent cystitis and bladder stones.

NATIONAL PERCENTAGES OF MEN WHO SIT DOWN TO PEE 'EVERY' OR 'MOST TIMES'

- **62%** GERMANY
- **50%** SWEDEN
- **44%** DENMARK
- **39%** AUSTRALIA
- **35%** FRANCE
- **35%** CANADA
- **34%** SPAIN
- **34%** ITALY
- **27%** POLAND
- **24%** **GREAT BRITAIN**
- **23%** **USA**
- **21%** **MEXICO**
- **20%** **SINGAPORE**

A SHORT, SLIGHTLY CROOKED AND
ULTIMATELY UNIMPRESSIVE HISTORY
OF NAPOLEON'S PENIS

Napoleon's penis, which enjoys its own Wikipedia page, has passed through a lot of hands since its theft during his autopsy. Previous owners include the legendary bookdealer A. S. W. Rosenbach (1876-1952), who bought the 'mummified tendon taken from Napoleon's body during the post-mortem' from Maggs Bros, London, in 1924. In 1927 it was exhibited at New York City's Museum of French Art, where a *Time* journalist compared it to a 'maltreated strip of buckskin shoelace', and another visitor thought it more like a 'shrivelled eel'. The humiliation continued with *The New York Times* describing it as 'barely recognisable as a human body part' in 2007, following the death of its owner John J. Lattimer (1914-2007), a New Jersey urologist. It was passed to his daughter, who has been offered $100,000 for it but is yet to sell.[54]

Dante Alighieri (*c.*1265-1321) once had a dramatic erotic dream about his unrequited love Beatrice that was so puzzling he wrote it as a sonnet and sent it to friends, appealing for their interpretation. In it, the Lord of Love appeared, taking Beatrice in his arms and feeding her his burning heart. One exasperated friend wrote back to him, advising Dante to 'give your balls/a good wash, so that the vapours/that make you talk nonsense/are extinguished and dispersed'. Dante grumbled that 'no one understood the true meaning of my dream.'

---

54. On the subject of Bonaparte genitalia, a curious fact about Napoleon's sister Pauline is that her voracious sexual appetite led to a diagnosis from her physicians of an 'exhausted vagina' from 'sexual overindulgence'. She liked to shock guests by changing in front of them, and wearing sheer dresses that revealed her rouged nipples.

The Great Singapore Penis Panic took place in 1967. Koro is a delusional disorder in which a person is overwhelmingly convinced that their sex organs are retracting and disappearing, despite physical evidence to the contrary. Listed in the *Diagnostic and Statistical Manual of Mental Disorders*, and also known as shrinking penis, cases have been reported around the world. ('Koro' is thought to derive from a Malay word for the head of a turtle or tortoise, used when referring to how it appears when it is retracted into the shell.) The most notable koro epidemic occurred in Singapore in October 1967. Newspapers initially reported a few cases of people suffering retracted genitals after eating pork from pigs dying of penile retraction, which immediately triggered a mass hysteria of koro cases over ten days. Singapore's General Hospital treated a total of 469 men and a dozen women frantic about their vanishing genitals. Actual physical injuries were suffered, by young men attempting to secure their penises in place using elastic bands, clamps and clothes pegs. A televised public health announcement had to be made to calm the populace.[55]

---

55. Incidentally a bit of a modern penis panic was caused in 2023 by a NASA-funded study by Justin D. La Favor and colleagues at Wake Forest University School of Medicine in North Carolina, who discovered that deep-space astronauts of the future will face significant problems with erectile dysfunction, caused by their exposure to cosmic rays and microgravity. As if they didn't have enough to worry about.*

   *On a related note, filmmakers in the adult film industry have been trying to film the first space pornography for years. An adult film actress named CoCo Brown began certification for co-piloting a Lynx spaceplane manufactured by XCOR, which was planned to take suborbital flight in 2016 and spend time in zero-gravity. Sadly, XCOR Aerospace declared bankruptcy before Miss Brown could complete her space pilot qualifications and take flight with her colleagues.

Truck nuts are vehicular vanity accessories imitating the human testicle sack that – it will come as no surprise – were invented in the USA in the 1980s, to butch up one's ride by attaching balls to one's bumper. Just who can claim credit for their invention is disputed, however. David Ham, founder of YourNutz.com, says he saw a custom pair at a rally in the 1980s and began making them in 1996. John D. Sallers, owner of BullsBalls.com, claims he got the idea when driving his 4×4 off-road and a passerby shouted, rather bafflingly: 'Go Ernie, show'em you got balls!', which gave him the idea and he began selling them in 2002. This led to what was actually termed in the press 'the Great Truck Nuts War', which rages on, despite the understandable efforts of various state legislatures to ban the display of human genitalia on the back of automobiles in public.

A pair of 'truck nuts', swinging freely.

Edward James (1907-1984), patron of the surrealists, was so besotted with his wife, the dancer Tilly Losch (1903-1975), that when he saw the trail of wet footprints she left up the stairs after her bath at Monkton House, England, he had them woven into the carpet. When the couple later divorced, he replaced them with the paw prints of his Irish Wolfhound.

Human breasts can leave unique identifiable patterns on surfaces as distinct as fingerprints. Even pairs of jeans have been used as forensic markers. Every pair of blue jeans displays a unique wear pattern, and in 1998 the FBI managed to use this fact to place a suspect at the scene of one of a spate of crimes in which criminals were robbing banks and detonating explosives in Spokane, Washington. Richard Vorder Bruegge, a forensic scientist at the FBI laboratory in Washington D.C., compared the jean pattern taken from 1996 footage of one of the masked men, with jeans owned by their list of suspects. In court, the man's defence team brought in a used-jeans exporter as an expert witness to argue the patterns were common, but with each of the thirty-four pairs of jeans he offered to the court to make his point the FBI team could still pick out the suspect's pair, and he was found guilty.

Humans glow in the dark. In fact, all living creatures emit a small amount of light produced by the chemical reactions occurring inside their bodies, but it was only in 2009 that Japanese scientists using ultrasensitive cameras managed to capture images of human bioluminescence.

Human beings also have invisible stripes, known as Blaschko lines, after the German dermatologist Alfred Blaschko (1858-1922), who discovered them in the early 1900s. The clue he followed was noticing how his patients' moles and rashes seemed to form linear patterns as though following invisible borders. As we grow from a single-cell organism, and our cells develop into muscles, bone and other parts of the body, the cells that form skin divide into groups that expand and spill against each other like milk poured into coffee – these pressing cellular swirls form our human tiger-stripes.

Contrary to popular belief, your skin's pores don't open or close – there is no muscle to make that happen. Their size doesn't change with the temperature of water with which you wash your skin; but they do start to naturally increase in size as you get older.

In France a dwarf named Richebourg (1756-1846), who was only 58cm tall, served as butler to the Duchess d'Orleans, mother of King Louis Philippe. After the first Revolution broke out he became a spy, smuggling dispatches abroad. This he did by dressing as a baby, carried in the arms of a nursemaid, with the messages hidden under his bonnet. The Orleans family provided him with a pension of 3000 francs, and he lived to the age of ninety in the Rue du Four St Germain.

During an otherwise unremarkable banquet thrown by the Duke of Buckingham in 1626 for Queen Henrietta Maria (1606-1669), wife of Charles I, out of a cold venison pie burst the 45cm-tall Jeffrey Hudson (1619-*c*.1682), wearing a miniature suit of armour and waving a sword. The Queen consort was so taken with the miniature seven-year-old child that Hudson soon moved into Denmark House as 'Lord Minimus, Queen's Dwarf', joining a menagerie of 'pets' that included a monkey called Pug and a Welsh giant named William Evans, who liked to pull a loaf from his pockets and make Hudson into a sandwich. Later in life, Hudson refused to humour any jokes about his modest dimensions. When in 1644 Charles Crofts, brother of the Queen's Master of Horse, made such a wisecrack, Hudson challenged him to a duel. Crofts arrived chuckling, carrying a 'squirt' (a large syringe full of water that used to serve as a fire extinguisher) for his weapon, to the amusement of the crowd. The 106cm Lord Minimus drew his pistol and shot him through the head.

One of the most extraordinary military units in history was the Potsdam Giants, a Prussian infantry regiment comprised entirely of unusually tall soldiers, no shorter than 1.9m. Founded in 1675 by Prince Frederick of Brandenburg (1657-1713), the regent selected only the tallest of the population to form his enormous contingent, even pairing the men with exceedingly tall women to breed giants.

Ferdinand Magellan (1480-1531) gave Patagonia its name (from *Patagão*, believed to mean 'Land of the Big Feet') after he and his crew encountered a race of giant people while exploring that coastline during their circumnavigation of the 1520s. Maps produced around this time carry the notation *regio gigantum* ('region of the giants'). Centuries later, in 1766, the British ship HMS *Dolphin*, captained by John 'Foul-Weather Jack' Byron (1723-1786) (grandfather of the poet), returned to London from a South American expedition reporting their own encounter with the enormous humanoid race. 'The existence of giants here is confirmed,' wrote Dr Matthew Maty, Secretary of the British Royal Society, in a letter to the French Academy of Sciences of that same year.

Macrophile (literally 'lovers of large') is the psychological term for a person – usually male – who has sexual fantasies about giants.

Researchers at the Department of Psychology at the University of North Florida found in 2015 that climbing a tall tree balancing on a beam for just a couple of hours can considerably improve cognitive and memory function.

Distant objects seem smaller when we look at them upside down. This was discovered by Professor Atsuki Higashiyama of Japan's Ritsumeikan University College of Letters, who published a study in 2006 about how the perceived size and distance of objects changed when he bent over and looked at them from between his legs.

You can be dyslexic in one language, but unimpaired in another. This was examined in a 2004 study at the University of Hong Kong, which drew on magnetic resonance imaging scans to show that the dyslexia of Chinese speakers occurred in different regions of the brain to those of dyslexic English speakers. So if you struggle with dyslexia in English, it's perfectly possible that it wouldn't be an issue in taking up a second language.

It was said of James IV of Scotland (1473-1513) that as an experiment in 1493 he sent two children to be raised by a mute woman alone on the island of Inchkeith, to see if they would develop language by themselves and thereby clarify whether language was innate or learned. It was claimed that the children began speaking excellent Hebrew, but even at the time these claims were treated with scepticism.

Holy Roman Emperor Frederick II (1194-1250) was also fond of experiments. According to a Franciscan named Salimbenedi Adam (1221-*c*.1290), Frederick wished to determine whether exercise or rest was better for digestion, and so he had two men fed well and sent one out hunting, while the other went to bed. He then had them killed and cut open to examine which had the clearer digestive system. The sleeper won, not that he was in much of a state to appreciate the information. Another tale told of Frederick is that he desired to examine the human soul, and so had a criminal nailed shut inside a barrel until he died. The idea was that when the barrel was opened before him, Frederick would see the trapped soul fly free. Alas, all the barrel contained was a needlessly suffocated corpse.

There was an experimental study published in 2015 about online therapy for chronic procrastinators, but the findings were inconclusive because 50 per cent of the participants didn't get around to completing the survey. The frustrated authors of *Experiences of Undergoing Internet-based Cognitive Behaviour Therapy for Procrastination: A qualitative study* grumbled that those participants seemed to 'lack motivation to complete the exercises, had too many conflicting commitments and were unable to keep up with the tight treatment schedule.'

SOME HISTORICAL PHOBIAS GATHERED FROM WHOLLY UNRELIABLE SOURCES

Erasmus (1469-1536) had such an aversion to fish that the smell of it threw him into a fever.

Ambrose Paré (1510-1590) mentions a gentleman who would fall into convulsions at the sight of a carp.

Władysław I Poland (1260/61-1333), King of Poland, known in English as the 'Elbow-high' or 'Ladislaus the Short', could not bear the sight of apples.

If an apple was shown to Chesne, secretary to Francis I of France (reigned 1515-1547), he bled at the nose. (Michel de Montaigne (1533-1592) wrote on this subject, that there were men who dreaded an apple more than a musket-ball.)

French Calvinist scholar Joseph Scaliger (1540-1609) was terrified of milk and turned pale at the sight of watercress. He also mentions one of his relations who experienced a similar horror upon seeing a lily.

Italian polymath Gerolamo Cardano (1501-1576) was profoundly disgusted by the sight of eggs; as was Alfred Hitchcock (1899-1980).

Henry III of France and Poland (1551-1589) could not sit in a room with a cat. Frederick Herman, Duke of Schomberg (1615-1693) had the same aversion, as did Napoleon I (1769-1821) and Adolf Hitler (1889-1945).

Pierre de Lancre (1553-1631), judge of Bordeaux, gives an account of an otherwise sensible man who was so terrified by hedgehogs that for two years he imagined his bowels were being gnawed by such an animal. De Lancre also knew of a battle-hardened army officer who was so fearful at the sight of a mouse that he never dared to look at one unless he had his sword in his hand.

The Portuguese physician Amatus Lusitanus (1511-1568) relates the case of a monk who fainted when he beheld a rose, and who would never leave his cell when the flowers were in bloom.

Hippocrates (*c*.460-*c*.375 BC) mentions a patient named Nicanor, who was put into 'a terrible fright' whenever he heard a flute.

Julia (1492-1542), daughter of Frederick, King of Naples, could not taste meat without 'serious accidents'.

Jean Louis de Nogaret de La Valette (1554-1642), Duke d'Epernon, was unfazed by the sight of hares, but when he was shown a leveret he fainted.

The Danish Renaissance astronomer Tycho Brahé (1546-1601) once fainted at the sight of a fox.[56]

Honoré d'Albert (1581-1649), Duke of Chaulnes, Marshal of France, Vidame of Amiens and Seigneur of Picquigny, once saw a pig and fainted.

The celebrated Pietro d'Abano (1257-1316), who professed, and exercised with great distinction, the practice of medicine at Bologne, was unable to look at, or even smell, cheese without fainting.

56. Which is particularly curious as he had no such aversion to his pet moose, which his biographer Pierre Gassendi tells us died after it 'had ascended the castle stairs and drunk of the beer in such amounts that it had fallen down [them].'

Martin Schoock (1614-1669), professor of philosophy at the University of Groningen, was under the same misfortune; and it induced him to write a 1664 treatise on the subject, *Accessit ejusdem Diatriba de aversatione casei* ('On the Dislike of Cheese').

The French philosopher Pierre Bayle (1647-1706) was seized with convulsions whenever he heard the noise of water falling from a rain spout. Bayle also writes of the case of an acquaintance who was horrified by honey: 'Without his knowledge, some honey was introduced in a plaster applied to his foot, and the accidents that resulted compelled his attendants to withdraw it.'

Sigmund Freud was afraid of ferns.

Walt Disney had a fear of mice.

Barack Obama has a fear of snowmen.

Eminem has a fear of owls.

The Procrastinators' Club of America was founded in 1956 in Philadelphia, Pennsylvania, with the stated purpose of promoting 'the philosophy of relaxation through putting off until later those things that needn't be done today'. By 2011 the club had grown to 12,000 members. In the past the group's activities have included an anti-war demonstration held in 1966 against the War of 1812, and a picket of the Whitechapel Bell Foundry, who cast the famously cracked Liberty Bell, with members holding signs like 'We got a lemon' and 'What about the warranty?' (The foundry offered to replace the bell if it was returned in its original packaging.) In 1976 the long-delayed opening of Philadelphia's Betsy Ross Bridge earned it the club's prestigious 'Award to Come Later' award.

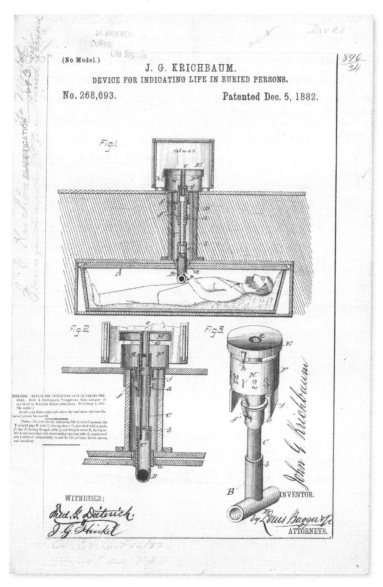

Patent drawing for J. G. Krichbaum's Device for Indicating Life in Buried Persons, *5 December 1882.*

The Victorians were terrified of being buried alive. Inventors came up with all sorts of preventative devices. The patent shown on the previous page is an example of a 'safety coffin', allowing a buried person to signal their still-breathing status from 1.8m under. The first example of this 'just-in-case' tomb-building philosophy was made in 1790 by Duke Ferdinand of Brunswick (1735-1806), whose coffin featured an air tube, a window and keys to the coffin lid and tomb placed in a pocket of his burial shroud. Dr Johann Gottfried Taberger's 1829 design had ropes tied to the corpse's hands, feet and head, all tethered to an above-ground bell. Should the bell ring, a servant was supposed to run over and start pumping air into the coffin. Other versions used firecrackers, rockets and flags, but quite often the designers did not take into consideration the fact that the body bloats and shifts during decomposition, and so more than a few false alarms were had.[57]

In February 2017, Chinese media reported that six officials of the Hubei province had been punished for falling asleep during a meeting to discuss how to motivate lazy bureaucrats. The Communist Party discipline bureau named the mid-level officials and said that they would be made to write self-criticisms and make public apologies.

In 1907 New York City socialite Ida Wood (1838-1932) announced that she was 'tired of everything'. She took out $1 million (about $30 million today) from her bank and went to live as a recluse in room 552 of the Herald Square Hotel with her two sisters. Twenty-four years later she left the room for the first time, to ask for a doctor.

---

57. Sean Connery was a professional coffin-polisher.

One of the longest diaries ever written is that of the chronically unsuccessful Boston poet Arthur Crew Inman (1895-1963), once described by *Time* magazine as a 'megalomaniacal bigot misogynist Peeping Tom hypochondriac' in a review of his 17-million-word, 155-volume journal. Debilitated by hypochondria, Inman vented an unceasing stream of irritability in his diaries while living in dark, soundproofed apartments. A typical excerpt: 'A Lithuanian came to read to me. I disliked her at once. She was common. Her voice sounded like an ungreased axle.' Inman's is one of the longest diaries in the English language. 'I trust to do in nonfiction what Balzac did in fiction,' he once said. Begun in 1919, the diary tracks every moment of his life until 1963, when he found the construction noise of the nearby Prudential Tower so unbearable that he shot himself with a revolver.[58]

The first object to be sent through the first pneumatic tube mail delivery system in 1897 was a Bible, at the Produce Exchange Building, New York City, USA. Shortly after went the second object: a live tortoiseshell cat.

---

58. A rival diary in size is that of Robert Shields (1918-2007), an American former minister and high-school English teacher, whose entries are somehow even less riveting, documenting every five minutes of his life from 1972 to 1997. Shields's volumes were donated to Washington State University following his death in 2007, along with a collection of his nose hair that he left behind in the hope it would be useful for 'further study'.

In April 1879, at the age of forty-three, a French postman named
Ferdinand Cheval (1836-1924) began building his Ideal Palace
at Hauterives, France, using pebbles he picked up each during his
delivery rounds. He finished thirty-three years later. The interior is
covered with Cheval's original quotes, such as: 'This is of art, and of
energy', 'The ecstasy of a beautiful dream and the prize of effort' and
'Out of a dream I have brought forth the Queen of the World'.

Ferdinand Cheval's homemade Ideal Palace.

Pliny the Elder credits the invention of writing to Menes (*fl. c.*3200-3000BC), an ancient Egyptian pharaoh of the Early Dynastic Period and unifier of Upper and Lower Egypt. We learn that this pharaoh had a love of riding crocodiles, but to the surprise of everyone this was not the cause of his untimely demise – Menes was instead seized and killed by a hippopotamus.

Charles Waterton (1782-1865) was an English naturalist, explorer and taxidermist. A noted eccentric, he was said to often dress like a scarecrow and sit in trees, pretend to be his own butler and tickle guests with a coal brush, or pretend to be a dog and bite his visitors. While wandering around Guyana he caught a crocodile by jumping on its back and riding it while pulling its forearms back. When it was exhausted, he tied a rope around its snout.

The phrase 'crocodile tears', meaning an insincere display of emotion, originates in an ancient story spread by writers like Plutarch (46-after 119) and later in English by Sir John Mandeville (*fl.*1356). Crocodiles were said to weep for their victims. By the time Edward Topsell (1572-1625) was perpetuating the myth in *The History of Four-footed Beasts* (1607), the crocodile was now doing it as a form of deception: 'Crocodili, lachrymae, the Crocodiles tears, justifieth the nature of this Beast, for there are not many brute beasts that can weep, but such is the nature of the crocodile that, to get a man within his danger, he will sob, sigh and weep as though he were in extremity, but suddenly he destroyeth him.'

Crocodiles do have tear ducts, and caymans and alligators have been observed emitting tears while they eat. This is thought to be due to their excited hissing, which forces air through their sinuses and is expelled through the tear glands.[59]

Thirteenth-century Europeans believed in a sea above the sky based on a misinterpretation of Genesis 1:7 – 'And God made the firmament, and divided the waters which were under the firmament from the waters which were above the firmament: and it was so.' The English author Gervase of Tilbury (*c*.1150-1220) recounts in his *Otia Imperialia* ('Recreation for an Emperor'), created *c*.1214 for his patron, Emperor Otto IV, the story of a ship's anchor falling from the sky and crashing into an unspecified English churchyard. As startled churchgoers gathered, a sky-sailor slid down the line from an aerial ship. The villagers managed to capture him, but he 'drowned' on the ground and his sky-shipmates abandoned him.

The earliest unidentified flying object (UFO) sighting dates back to Ancient Rome: 'Something that looked like ships gleamed down from the sky ... Something that looked like a big fleet was said to have been seen in the sky at Lanuvium, near Rome' (quoted by Livy in *History of Rome* 21.62 and 42.2 from official lists of *prodigia*, or unusual occurrences).

---

59. Research published in August 2023 in *Proceedings of the Royal Society B: Biological Sciences* showed that, while the cries of human infants might stir protective maternal instincts in other species, to Nile crocodiles the sound of a crying baby was akin to 'a dinner bell', triggering their predatory instincts.

By the sixteenth century the compass needle's draw to the north was explained with the mythological belief in the Rupes Nigra, a giant, magnetic, black mountain surrounded by a swirling vortex and lands of Arctic pygmies at the North Pole. The most famous early mapping of this is by Gerardus Mercator (1512-1594) as a vignette on his world map of 1569. The cartographer explained the idea to the astrologer and mathematician John Dee (1527-1608) in 1577: 'Right under the Pole there lies a bare Rock in the midst of the Sea. Its circumference is almost 33 miles, and it is all of magnetic Stone.'

In 1822 a confidence trickster invented a country and pulled off one of the greatest financial scams committed. 'Sir' Gregor MacGregor (1786-1845), whose knighthood was self-bestowed, was a renowned Scottish soldier who strode into London and announced that he'd been given some 3.3 million hectares of South American territory by the King of the Mosquito Coast to form a new country that he was calling Poyais. Investment in the initiative was open to all. For a mere two shillings and three pence, MacGregor told his rapt audience, a 0.4-hectare parcel of paradise territory could be theirs. This meant that, if they were able to scrape together £11, they could own a plot of 40 hectares. Families purchased prestigious positions in Poyais government and military for their young men and women, and hundreds of settlers purchased tickets on ships to the new land, transferring all their money into Poyais dollars. The entire scheme was a con, no such territory had been allocated, and MacGregor escaped with the equivalent of over £3.6 billion sterling. He fled to Venezuela, where he was buried with full military honours in Caracas Cathedral in 1845.

A bank note produced for the nonexistent country of Poyais.

George C. Parker (1860-1936) was a spectacular American con artist whose specialty was selling public landmarks to gullible buyers. He was particularly fond of selling Brooklyn Bridge to investors, who would immediately erect toll booths on the bridge, which had to be cleared away by police more than once. Parker's ambitiously imaginative property portfolio also included Madison Square Garden, the Metropolitan Museum of Art, Grant's Tomb (which he sold by pretending to be the grandson of Ulysses S. Grant) and the Statue of Liberty. He was convicted three times for fraud, escaping one sentencing in 1908 by simply putting on a sheriff's hat and coat and walking out of the building. His exploits are why we have the expression 'and if you believe that, I have a bridge to sell you'.

🏛️

One rare series of banknote sought by collectors is the 2-, 100-, 500- and 1000-rupee notes issued by the State Bank of Nepal in 1981. In these, a small but considerable graphic error was made with a line extending from the lower lip of the King of Nepal, which gives the instant impression that the King is dribbling.

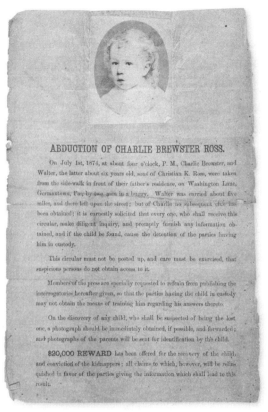

The first photographic 'wanted poster'.

The first 'wanted poster' with a photograph was for a four-year-old boy. On 1 July 1874 Charley Brewster Ross was abducted with his six-year-old brother Walter in Philadelphia. Walter was left behind by the kidnappers, but Charley was taken in what was the first American kidnapping for ransom. When the police ran out of leads, the parents hired Allan Pinkerton of the Pinkerton National Detective Agency to find him. Pinkerton devised the posters and handed them out to the public in the hopes it would lead to a tip-off, but poor Charley Brewster Ross was never found, and his fate remains unknown.

A less well-known detail about the authors of *The Communist Manifesto* (1848) is that Karl Marx (1818-1883) and Friedrich Engels (1820-1895) were both shrewd investors on the London Stock Exchange. Marx came into some money in 1864, when he was left £820 by an admirer. In a letter to his uncle Lion Philips of that summer Marx writes: 'I have, which will surprise you not a little, been speculating ... in English stocks, which are springing up like mushrooms this year ... and are forced up to quite an unreasonable level and then, for the most part, collapse. In this way, I have made over £400 ...'. Engels, meanwhile, retired in 1869 from a successful business career that included a seat on a stock exchange, with an investment portfolio of blue-chip stocks worth about £1.2 million in today's currency. When he died twenty-six years later, his shares in the London and Northern Railway Co., South Metropolitan Gas Co., Channel Tunnel Corp. and Foreign and Colonial Government Trust Co. and others were worth the equivalent of £2.2 million.

At the peak of hyperinflation in Germany in 1923, one loaf of bread had increased in price from 163 marks in 1922 to 200,000 million marks by late 1923. The exchange rate for US$1 was one to 1000 billion German marks.

Today, US currency is mandated to carry the official motto 'In God We Trust', but the first official US coin in circulation, the Fugio cent of 1787, carried the motto 'Mind Your Business'.

A Romanian banknote of 10,000 lei was released in 1994, featuring a statue of an ancient snake deity called Glycon that had been discovered in 1962 during excavation beneath the former Pallas railway station in Constanța, Romania. The cult of the snake god Glycon was founded by Alexander of Abonoteichos (*c*.105-*c*.170), a Greek mystic and/or con artist who used a hand puppet in the form of a serpent to convince his followers that he was the prophet of the deity and could divine the future.

Fāl-gūsh is a Persian form of divination in which you stand in a hidden spot like a dark corner or behind a fence and eavesdrop on strangers' conversations. You then find ways of applying the overheard words and sentences as answers to your own questions.

SOME CURIOUS METHODS
OF TELLING THE FUTURE

Abacomancy
observing patterns in dust

Alectryomancy
observing the behaviour of roosters

Amniomancy
reading a baby's placenta

Apantomancy
interpreting encounters with animals or objects

Armomancy
reading one's own shoulders or the shoulder blades of an animal

Cephaleonomancy
boiling a donkey or goat head

Cromniomancy
examining onion sprouts

Dictiomancy
opening a dictionary at random

Gastromancy
listening to the gurgling sounds of the digestive system

Geloscopymancy
analysing a person's laughter

Gyromancy

recording the letters that a dizzy person falls upon

Hyomancy

observing the behaviour of wild hogs

Maculomancy

analysing spots on the skin

Margaritomancy

casting pearls, or examining pearls in oysters

Ololygmancy

divining the howling of dogs

Ptarmoscopy

interpreting sneezes

Scarpomancy

studying old shoes

Scatomancy

examining a person's excrement

Symbolomancy

finding meaning in random things discarded on the road

Tyromancy/tiromancy

telling the future by examining cheese

Urticariaomancy

telling the future by analysing itches

In Ancient Rome it was the job of members of the College of Augurs to interpret the will of the gods by watching the southern sky for lightning bolts. If lightning flashed from left to right it was a favourable omen. If lightning strikes were spotted, the magistrates of Rome were required to cancel any public assemblies arranged for the following day.

The average bolt of lightning carries 100 million volts and can instantly reach a temperature of 27,760°C.

Before the invention of the lightning rod, tall churches and castles were extremely dangerous places to be in thunderstorms. Bell ringers in Europe were frequent casualties thanks to the belief that the clamour of bells would ward off the evil spirits trying to attack the church with lightning. (This is why the inscription *Fulgura frango* is often found etched on bells of this period, with its meaning 'I break up the lightning flashes.') In France for example, between 1753 and 1786, lightning struck 386 French church towers, with current arcing down the bell ropes killing 103 French bell ringers. In 1786 the French government finally outlawed the custom of bell ringing in thunderstorms.

But the real danger was in the habit of storing gunpowder in the vaults of castles and churches. Athlone Castle, Ireland, was hit by a lightning bolt on 27 October 1697 that detonated 260 barrels of gunpowder with a blast that obliterated the building and much of the surrounding town ('None Killed of Note …', commented one contemporary account). In 1769 a bolt hit the Church of St Nazaire in Brescia, northern Italy, where nearly 100 tonnes of gunpowder were stored. The ensuing explosion killed 3000 people and destroyed one-sixth of the city.

The magnetic compass was originally used for fortune-telling. On its invention in China during the Han Dynasty (between the second century BC and early third century AD), the 'south-governor' as it was called was a tool of geomancers – fortune-tellers who performed divinations by scattering sand or soil and interpreting the patterns. Practitioners of feng shui also employed it for building structures in harmony with their environment. From what we can tell, it was between the ninth and eleventh centuries when Chinese navigators incorporated the compass as a navigational instrument; while in Europe we find the first reference to such a device in Alexander Neckam's *De Naturis Rerum* ('On the Nature of Things') produced in 1190.

In 1778, following Benjamin Franklin's invention of the lightning rod, a craze for 'lightning rod fashion' took Paris by storm. Women wore *le chapeau paratonnerre* ('the lightning hat'), with conductive metal ribbon and chain running from the hat to the ground; while men strutted around with *le parapluie-paratonnerre* (the 'lightning umbrella'), with an extended metal tip to act as a rod, with chain running down to the floor.

A curious Victorian myth to do with lightning appeared with the arrival of photography. Keraunography was the nineteenth-century belief that lightning functioned like a camera flash, and that people and animals struck by it were imprinted with a photographic image of their surroundings. The myth originated from early legends of the 1300s to the 1600s in which people hit by lightning in churches were said to have been etched with crosses; and from the fact that lightning burns do take patterned forms. The myth is hinted at by the modern term 'keraunographic marks' for the scars left by lightning on the human body, which are also known as 'lightning flowers'.

THE SEVEN STRIKES OF ROY SULLIVAN, 'LIGHTNING RANGER'

It seems unlikely that there has ever been an unluckier person than Roy Cleveland Sullivan (1912-1983), a US park ranger in Shenandoah National Park in Virginia. Between 1942 and 1977, Sullivan was hit by lightning on seven different occasions. This earned him the nickname of the 'Human Lightning Rod', and recognition by Guinness World Records as the person struck by lightning more recorded times than any other person in history.

STRIKE #1: April 1942. Sullivan is hiding from a thunderstorm in a fire lookout tower when it's hit multiple times and begins to catch fire. So far unscathed, he runs out of the building to escape the flames and is struck by a lightning bolt that scorches a 1.3cm strip down his right leg and leaves a hole in his shoe.

STRIKE #2: July 1969. While driving on a mountain road a lightning bolt misses his truck and strikes trees nearby. Unfortunately, the lightning is then deflected through the open window of his vehicle and hits Sullivan, knocking him unconscious and scorching off his hair, eyebrows and eyelashes. His truck comes to a rest on a cliff edge.

STRIKE #3: In 1970, while standing in his front yard, a lightning bolt hits a nearby power transformer and leaps to his left shoulder, leaving a severe burn.

STRIKE #4: In 1972, Sullivan is working in a ranger station in Shenandoah National Park when the station is hit and his hair is lit on fire. He tries to put out the flames with his jacket, which doesn't work, so he runs to the toilet, but can't fit his head under the tap, and so soaks a towel and wraps it around his head. Though not previously superstitious, he is now convinced some unseen force is trying to kill him, and becomes paranoid, carrying a can of water with him everywhere and avoiding crowds of people for fear of bringing harm to them.

STRIKE #5: In 1973, while out on patrol, Sullivan sees a storm cloud forming and speeds away in the opposite direction. But the cloud, he would later swear, starts to pursue him. When he feels like he's finally outrun it, he cautiously steps out of his truck and is immediately struck by a lightning bolt. His hair is again set on fire as the bolt tears down his left arm, leg and blows off his shoe, before crossing to scorch his right leg below the knee. He crawls to his truck, grabs the can of water he takes everywhere with him, and pours it over his head.

STRIKE #6: In 1976, he tries to flee another thunderstorm, but is struck again and injures his ankle. His hair also catches fire.

STRIKE #7: In 1977, Sullivan is fishing in a freshwater pool when lightning strikes the top of his head, burning his hair, chest and stomach. As he staggers to his car, his misfortune continues – a bear approaches and tries to grab the trout from his fishing line. Sullivan manages to hit the bear with a tree branch and scare it away. He later revealed that this was the twenty-second time he had had to beat away a bear with a stick.[60]

Marchesa Luisa Casati (1881-1957) in 1922. A figure of the belle époque and muse of surrealist and futurist artists including Man Ray, Casati endeavoured to be a 'living work of art' and collected wax likenesses of herself in wigs of her own hair. In anticipation of an upcoming high-society event, she commissioned the costume designer of the Ballets Russes to create her a dress covered in tiny electric bulbs. Her wish to make an impression was granted – the electric dress short-circuited and gave her such a terrific shock that the blast caused her to somersault backwards.

60. Six per cent of Americans believe that they could defeat a grizzly bear in unarmed combat.

When the engine of his F-8 fighter jet stalled and the auxiliary power lever broke off in his hand on 26 July 1959 at 1800hrs, US Marine aviator Lieutenant Colonel William Rankin (1920-2009) ejected without a pressure suit at 14,300m into air temperatures of -50°C, immediately suffering frostbite and decompression injuries. Five minutes after abandoning his plane his parachute had not yet opened, and he was somehow still falling – he had ejected into a cumulonimbus thunderstorm cloud. At 3000m his parachute finally opened but updrafts kept dragging him back up through the cloud (a phenomenon known as 'cloud suck'), as hailstones pummelled him and winds spun him around violently. He was surrounded by so much rain that he had to hold his breath so as not to drown. When he finally came to land in a forest, exhausted and bleeding, the time was 1840hrs – he had 'fallen' for forty minutes.

How much does a cloud weigh? In 2003 Peggy LeMone, an atmospheric scientist at the National Center for Atmospheric Research in Boulder, Colorado, USA, decided to calculate the weight of an average cumulus cloud. By estimating the density of water droplets at ½g per cu. m, she came up with an average weight of around 550 tons of water. This is, she pointed out, approximately the same as the weight of 100 elephants, suspended above your head. Using the same method, LeMone was also able to calculate that the weight of the average hurricane is equal to 40 million elephants.

The winds of the average hurricane produce about 1.5 trillion watts, which is enough to power half the world for an entire year.

SOME INSTANCES OF NON-AQUEOUS RAIN

*A shower of snakes during a rainstorm, reported in the
natural wonder compendium* Der Wunder-reiche Uberzug
unserer Nider-Welt … *(1680) by Erasmus Francisci.*

582 St Gregory of Tours (538/539-594) records: 'In the territory
of Paris there rained real blood from the clouds, falling upon the
garments of many men, who were so stained and spotted that they
stripped themselves of their own clothing in horror.' (Perhaps rain
carrying red dust from the Sahara.)

1794 French soldiers witness huge numbers of toads tumbling
from the sky amid a heavy rainstorm at Lalain, near Lille.

Woodcut by Hans Glaser (c.1500-1573) depicting a blood rain that occurred near Dinkelsbühl on 26 May 1554.

1804 Professor Pontus of Cahors, near Toulouse, reports to the *Academie francaise* that a thunderstorm has left roads and fields covered with frogs four-deep, which clogged the wheels of his carriage.

1827 *Journal of St Petersbourg* reports that at Pakroff in Russia an early snowfall was accompanied by a tremendous shower of unidentified black insects over 2.5cm in length, which seemed to prefer the cold, as they quickly died if brought inside.

1861 French naturalist Francis de Laporte de Castelnau (1802-1880) concludes that a recent fish-rain in Singapore could be explained by a migration of walking catfish that somehow dragged themselves over land from one puddle to the next.

1876 On 3 March the incident known as the Kentucky Meat Shower occurs, in which 10cm chunks of red meat fall from the sky across Olympian Springs in Bath County, Kentucky. The leading explanation is that it was the result of a flock of vultures passing overhead that threw up their meals after being startled.

2000 On 8 August a shoal of sprat rains down on Great Yarmouth, Norfolk, following a thunderstorm.

2004 Fish fall from the sky above the Welsh market town of Knighton, Powys.

2007 'Large tangled clumps of worms' fall on the town of Jennings, Louisiana, possibly deposited by a water spout that had touched down 8km away. 'I looked in the sky, there was no clouds,' according to Jennings Police Department employee Eleanor Beal. 'I said, "It's worms! Get out of the way!"' [61]

---

61. A special mention should be made here to an occurrence annually remembered in Chicago that took place on 8 August 2004, known as the Dave Matthews Band Chicago River incident. At 1.18 p.m. on the hot summer's day, as the rock band's tour bus was crossing the Kinzie Street bridge, the bus driver decided to dump the estimated 360kg of human waste from the bus's blackwater tank onto the metal grates of the bridge, to fall into the Chicago river. Unfortunately, at that exact moment an open-topped sightseeing boat full of tourists was passing below. It was a direct hit. The band was fined $200,000. The boat's crew swabbed the deck and resumed service for the 3 p.m. tour.

Every summer the inhabitants of Yoro, Honduras, hold a festival called the *Festival de Lluvia de Peces* ('festival of the fish rain') to celebrate the annual phenomenon of fish falling from the sky, which, it is claimed, can occur as often as four times a year.

As much as half of all the water on Earth may have originated as ice specks floating in an interstellar gas cloud in existence before our solar system. This means that there's a 50:50 chance that the water in your glass is older than the Sun.

In the Gulf of Mexico and other places around the world, there are lakes on the sea floor. When seawater dissolves thick layers of salt beneath the sea floor, the layers collapse and form depressions. These are then filled with water made denser by the dissolved salt, which form their own lakes and rivers.

The Ordnance Survey, the British mapping agency, bases its every elevation, contour line and spot height in its maps on a single brass bolt screwed into the floor of a small hut at the end of a pier in Newlyn, Cornwall. Between 1915 and 1921, the distance of the bolt head from the sea level was measured every hour, until a mean sea level was established. This remains the reference for sea level, though modern lasers and satellites have of course helped enhance things: in 2016, for example, Ben Nevis grew by 1m on paper, as it was discovered that it was slightly taller than previously thought.

The earliest photograph of a surfer, from *c*.1898, by Frank Davey (1860-1922). The Hawaiian surfer Charles Kauha wears the malo at Waikiki Beach and carries one of the last Alaia surfboards.

American adventurer Paul Boyton (*c*.1848-1924) tests an inflatable life-preserving rubber suit in the Atlantic, after sneaking on board an American steamer bound for Ireland and leaping overboard in it when the coastline came into view. The suit featured a little foghorn, and a sail attached to the foot.

One of the tales told of Alexander the Great (356-323 BC) is of him being lowered into the sea inside an airtight barrel to explore subaquatic wonders. Inside he's accompanied by a cockerel to tell the time, and a cat whose breath purifies the air. From the *Roman d'Alexandre* (1444-1445).

This is the earliest known illustration of a diving suit, from Conrad Kyeser's (1366-1405) *Bellifortis*, an illustrated manuscript on military technology finished shortly before his death. Two men face off underwater, with a Latin inscription revealing that it's a suit of armour lined with sponge, with eyepieces of glass.

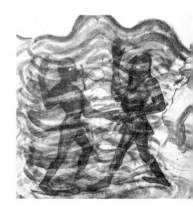

Naumachiae were giant sea battles re-enacted in deliberately flooded Roman arenas. Condemned criminals and captured prisoners of war fought to the death as they played out famous naval campaigns for the entertainment of a crowd. Natural settings such as lakes and the Rhegium coast were used; but there is also evidence to suggest that the battles were hosted in amphitheatres. For years archaeologists have debated whether the dual-level labyrinth of chambers beneath the Coliseum arena known as the *hypogea* support or disprove the notion that aquatic displays were staged in the arena in Rome. Ancient sources indicate that *naumachiae* did indeed take place, but it is thought that for this to have been successful the ships involved must have been smaller in scale. This is especially likely when one takes into consideration the fact that the length of one trireme was nearly half the length of the entire Coliseum amphitheatre. The Coliseum, or the Flavian Amphitheatre as it is also known, is thought to have housed these spectacles on its launch.[62]

There has been a wild variety of proposals to raise the *Titanic*. These include filling the shipwreck with ping-pong balls for buoyancy; pumping it with 180,000 tonnes of Vaseline; and blasting the wreck with 0.5 million tonnes of liquid nitrogen (and irony) to turn its fragile remains into an iceberg that would float to the surface. One of the most eccentric sponsors of expeditions to find the wreck was the

---

62. Today we're using great quantities of water for depressingly less spectacular purposes. In 2023 Alex de Vries at the VU Amsterdam School of Business and Economics in the Netherlands calculated that a single bitcoin transaction uses 16,000 litres of clean water, which is involved in producing the electricity required, and the cooling of the hardware used.

Texan oilman Jack Grimm (1925-1998), who had also led searches
for Noah's Ark, the Loch Ness Monster, Bigfoot and the giant hole
in the North Pole that was part of the Hollow Earth theory. His
research vessel *HJW Fay* departed Port Everglades, Florida, on
17 July 1980 after an initial delay caused by Grimm's insistence that
they use a monkey trained to point to where the *Titanic* lay on a map.
Grimm grudgingly backed down when the science team told him it
was either them or the monkey.

On 9 August 1996 during the filming of the James Cameron movie
Titanic in Halifax, Nova Scotia, 150 members of the cast and crew
were rushed to hospital when it was realised that the chowder
provided by the set catering staff had been heavily dosed with the
hallucinogenic drug PCP, also known as 'angel dust'. About half an
hour after the group meal, all hell had broken loose. James Cameron
was seen running with an extra to the toilet to make himself throw
up, shouting 'There's something in me! Get it out!' According to
the set decorator Claude Roussel, 'Bill Paxton was sitting next to
me in the hallway of the hospital, and he was kind of enjoying the
buzz. Meanwhile, grips were going down the hallway doing wheelies
in wheelchairs.' Cameron also recalled the scene at the hospital:
'People are moaning and crying, wailing, collapsed on tables and
gurneys. The DP [director of photography], Caleb Deschanel, is
leading a number of crew down the hall in a highly vocal conga line.'
The culprit was never identified.

The largest cruise ship in the world, Royal Caribbean's
Wonder of the Seas, is so big that its passenger capacity
is more than the population of the City of London.

The Floating Church of the Redeemer of Philadelphia was an
aquatic church conceived in 1847 by the Churchmen's Missionary
Association for Seamen, which had it built on two 27m-long, 100-
ton barges. It sailed around the Delaware river to attend to the needs
of mariners in its various ports.

When the third Ming Emperor Yongle (1360-1424) rose to power
in China in 1402, he appointed his favourite eunuch Zheng He
(pronounced *jung-huh*) (1371-1433) to command an enormous
expeditionary force to the South Pacific and Indian Oceans. Never
has there been a spectacle of such might as the colossal Chinese fleet
of Admiral Zheng He, considered China's greatest explorer. In seven
voyages over twenty years, Zheng He opened up much of south and
western Asia, and even east Africa to his traditionally insular nation.
He did this with ships of massive size, giant treasure-ship junks
accompanied by an armada of smaller vessels. Reputedly the largest
of these ships had four decks and measured 137m long and 55m
at the beam, the widest part of a ship. The British sinologist Joseph
Needham (1900-1995) considered this to be a conservative figure,
estimating the length to be closer to 120-180m.[63]

To put these measurements in context, this is twice the width and
just over half the length of the *Titanic* (at 28m wide and 269m
long). The vessels would also have completely dwarfed Christopher
Columbus's (1451-1506) largest ship, *Santa María*; in fact, if you
took every ship involved in the explorations of Columbus and Vasco
da Gama (*c*.1460-1524), you'd be able to fit them all on the top deck
of just one of Zheng He's treasure ships.

---

63. These sizes have been contested on the grounds of sheer impracticability, and while
there is to be expected a degree of hyperbole to such legend it is interesting to note that
two of the dry docks at Longjiang, where the ships would have been built, were 64m
wide, sufficient for the construction of vessels of such monstrous dimensions.

Olaf Tryggvason (*c*.964-*c*.1000), King of Norway, is described as 'frolicsome, gay and social … and very violent in all respects' in the Icelandic sagas, which also note that Olaf liked to run around the outside of his Viking vessel on the oars of his men as they rowed at sea.

Viking games were unsurprisingly brutal. From the Icelandic sagas we learn various details of what they did for pleasure, like the game *hnútukast*, in which one attempted to kill an opponent by hurling bones at their head as hard as possible. *Sköfuleikr* was pretty to similar to *hnútukast*, except that you threw pot scrapers made from cow horn. *Sund* was a kind of underwater wrestling in which you tried to drown your friend; and there was also a form of tug-of-war played over an open fire, in which you both stood naked and tugged on an animal skin to try and pull your opponent into the flames.

30 FASTEST 100M SPRINT TIMES

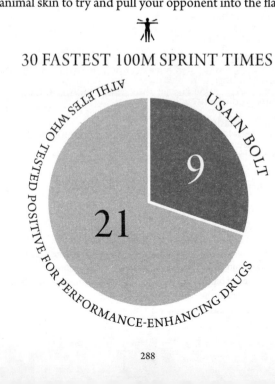

The 1900 Olympiad featured an experimental programme of tug-of-war, pigeon racing, hot-air-balloon target-bombing, kite-flying, cricket, equestrian long jump and competitive firefighting. The swimming obstacle race and the competitive lifesaving event were held in the river Seine. Only the French players turned up to compete in the croquet competition, and only one paying spectator attended: an Englishman, who had made the trip specially from Nice.

The forgotten revolutionary of American baseball was an Englishman named Charles Howard Hinton (1853-1907), a brilliant mathematician who coined the term 'tesseract'.[64] In 1897, while teaching at Princeton University, he wrote an article in *Harper's Weekly* laying out his invention of the first baseball pitching machine: 'It occurred to me that practically whenever men wished to impel a ball with velocity and precision, they drove it out of a tube with powder. Following then the course of history, I determined to use a cannon of a bore which would just hold a baseball ...' His machine consisted of a breech-loading rifle action, with a brass tube for a barrel, made telescopic to allow for variation in velocity. Unfortunately, he ran into several problems, the main one being that people don't like being shot at. The cannon terrified the batters, who instinctively learned to dive out of the way when it was fired. Also, the gunpowder blast had a tendency to cook and harden the leather surface of the ball so that after a couple of 'pitches' it had all the

---

64. After graduating from Balliol College, Oxford, Hinton taught at Uppingham School until he was convicted of bigamy and forced to find new employment. This behaviour was no doubt influenced by the example set by his polygamist father, who once told Hinton's mother: 'Christ was the saviour of Men but I am the saviour of Women and I don't envy him one bit.'

elasticity of a flying brick. The device was too far ahead of its time. Hinton was forced to concede defeat and the invention was retired.

MECHANICAL PITCHER—EXPERIMENTAL FORM.

An early iteration of Hinton's baseball cannon.

On the night of 9 October 1971 heavy rain fell unexpectedly on the courts before the finals of the 1971 Davis Cup competition in Charlotte, North Carolina, USA. Officials brought in a low-flying helicopter to help dry out the courts and, when that didn't work, as a last resort they soaked the courts with gasoline and lit a match.[65]

---

65. Since we've ventured into the theme of ignition here, allow me to cram in an interesting thing about the Russian Space Programme. In the 1950s Soviet engineers working on the first intercontinental missiles sought a way to ignite the device's multiple nozzles simultaneously. They invented the PZU, a Russian abbreviation for 'pyrotechnic ignition device', which is a wooden, T-shaped stick with wired pyro-charges at their tips, inserted manually into each nozzle. Detonated in concert, these ensure the engines ignite at the same time, and are still in use today. This means Russian rockets are essentially lit with giant matchsticks.

The invention of the roller-skate is credited to the eccentric Belgian engineer Joseph Merlin (1735-1803), who produced a variety of intricate machines, musical instruments and automata (including the stunning Silver Swan currently housed in England's Bowes Museum), but it was the disastrous debut of his wheeled shoe in 1760 that made his name. The writer Joseph Strutt (1749-1802) recounts recounts the events of the grand unveiling (*Sports and Pastimes*, 1801). Bear in mind as you read the following that, according to other sources, Monsieur Merlin was simultaneously playing the violin at the time:

> 'Joseph Merlin of Liege, who came to England with the Spanish ambassador in 1760, invented a pair of skates that ran on wheels. But his exhibition of them was not a success. Gliding about in them at a masquerade at Carlisle House, Soho Square, he ran into a valuable mirror worth £500, which he completely shattered in addition to wounding himself severely.'

Professor Crum Brown (1838-1922) was a respected lecturer in chemistry at the University of Edinburgh, whose hand once caught fire during a game of golf. Having the idea to invent a way of being able to play golf at night, he coated balls in a phosphorescent paint of his own devising that would make them impossible to lose and then went out into the night to play a round on a nearby course. The idea worked, but during the game he smelled smoke, and looked down to find his golfing glove in flames, having reacted with the chemical that coated the ball and spontaneously combusted.

Glow-in-the-dark golf balls are today used for night golf at one of the world's most unusual golf courses, at Coober Pedy Opal Fields, Australia, when the day's heat is too great for comfortable play. There's no grass at Coober Pedy; the fairways are white sand, and the greens are black, made by pouring motor oil onto the ground, which results in a smooth surface and prevents the sand from blowing away.

The greatest professional footballer to never play a professional match is Carlos Henrique Raposo (b.1963), known as Carlos Kaiser, a Brazilian player and con artist who managed to sign for numerous teams in Brazil, Argentina and France as a striker during a decade-long career, while never actually playing a game. The man who 'wanted to be a footballer but did not want to play football' would deliberately incur red cards as soon as he entered the pitch by fouling players or fighting with the crowd, and would feign injuries that were hard to disprove, like pulled hamstrings. If that didn't work, he had a local dentist confirm he had a focal infection. Meanwhile he would use dummy mobile phones to loudly reject other 'offers' from rival clubs and befriend journalists to write favourable pieces, all to maintain an artificially inflated profile.

Ancient Greek athletes sometimes tied up their penis for freer movement. The foreskin was pulled forward and trussed up with a cord called a *kynodesme*, which translates as 'dog leash'. [66]

---

66. No such equipment was needed at the 1851 Wenlock Olympics in Shropshire, England, by the way, which featured the Old Women's Race with the prize being 450g of tea and the hotly contested Stocking-Knitting competition.

Ski ballet is a forgotten sport that arose in the 1970s, and incorporated moves from figure skating, classical ballet and gymnastics, with the skier performing a 90-second routine set to music on a gentle slope. The choreography featured jumps, pole flips, rolls, leg-crossings, pole-twirling and spins while skiing, with the dancers all the while emoting to the strains of Chopin, Mozart and Huey Lewis and the News. One of the biggest ski ballet stars Suzanne 'Suzy Chapstick' Chaffee, a former Ford model and Olympic alpine skier whose trademark move was the eye-watering Suzy Split, in which she performed a complete forward split while balanced

Rune Kristiansen performs a routine on 12 March 1993 as part of a ski ballet competition, a sport now all but forgotten.

on the tips of her skis. Despite its inclusion as a demonstration sport at the 1988 and 1992 Olympics, ski ballet never gained the official recognition its supporters felt it deserved. The sport quickly faded away, leaving the world to check its drink and wonder whether the whole thing had been some kind of drug-induced hallucination.

The Greek geographer Pausanias (*fl.*143-176) wrote that women were forbidden from spectating at the ancient Olympic games and had to remain on the other side of the river Alpheus. If any women were caught watching, they should be thrown off a cliff.

Ancient Roman women didn't have first names. They were identified by the feminine of their family name, which could be differentiated with their father's name or their husband's name. If one of several siblings, a woman might have a numerical adjective such as Tertia (the Third) added too. Names like Aemilia, Cornelia and Claudia that are today used as first names were originally the family names of great patrician houses of Rome. Naming practices began to change only in the Late Antiquity period.

Lucius Licinius Crassus (140-91 BC), Roman orator and statesman, had a pet eel that he loved so much he gave it necklaces and earrings, and held a grand funeral when it died. When this was commented on sarcastically by his colleague Gnaeus Domitius Ahenobarbus (d.31 BC), Crassus replied: 'Did you not bury three wives and not shed a tear?'

'Putting goat dung in their diapers soothes hyperactive children, especially girls.' Pliny the Elder, *Natural History* 28.259.

Ancient Roman soldiers would refer to a military camp set up on hostile uneven ground as a *noverca*, which means 'stepmother'.

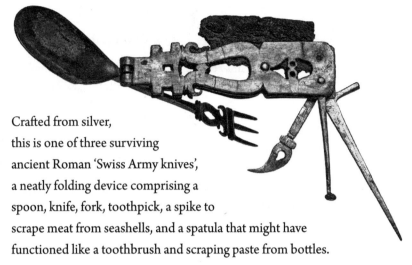

Crafted from silver,
this is one of three surviving
ancient Roman 'Swiss Army knives',
a neatly folding device comprising a
spoon, knife, fork, toothpick, a spike to
scrape meat from seashells, and a spatula that might have
functioned like a toothbrush and scraping paste from bottles.

'Lucius Verratius was an extremely evil and deranged fellow. He used to amuse himself by striking free men on the face with the palm of his hand. A slave would follow after him with a purse full of small coins. Whenever he had slapped anyone, he would tell the slave to count out twenty-five asses on the spot, as the compensation ordered by the *Twelve Tables*'. Aulus Gellius (*fl. c.*101-200), *Noctes Atticae* ('Attic Nights'): 20.1.13.

In Ancient Rome, a particularly risky job was that of the ornatrix servant girl, or hair stylist. Ovid (43BC-AD 17/18) in *Ars Amatoria* ('The Art of Love') feels forced to instruct women not to beat their hairdresser: 'May your hairdresser be safe; I hate the woman who claws her maid's face with her nails and stabs her arms with a snatched-up acus.'

Ancient Roman men had beauty standards to keep to, as well. Seneca (*c.*4 BC-AD 65) complains about the noise made by male bathers screaming as they have their armpit hair plucked by beauticians.

'Misopogonistic' is a rare adjective that means 'having a hatred of beards'; or more specifically, in the meaning of the Byzantine Greek word from which it derives, 'a hatred of bearded philosophers'. *The Misopogon*, or *Beard-Hater*, is an essay ostensibly mocking bearded philosophers, that actually satirises the people of Antioch, and was written by the Roman Emperor Julian (331/332-363) just before his death.

A 2006 US survey of hundreds of white-bearded shopping-mall Santas found that 34 per cent regularly had wet laps from being urinated on by children. Some 50 per cent said children tried to steal their glasses daily. Over 60 per cent said that children coughed or sneezed directly in their faces at least ten times per day, and 74 per cent said they had ten children crying on their laps each day. Around 90 per cent of working Saint Nicks have their beard yanked every day to see if it's real: 'Children can really put the wear and tear on you,' confirmed Timothy Connaghan, head of the Santa Association.

Jolabokaflod ('Christmas book flood') is an Icelandic tradition begun after the Second World War, when paper was one of the few things not rationed. Families give each other books as Christmas presents, which are opened on 24 December, so they can all read together that evening.

In Dutch tradition, Sinterklaas arrives by steamboat from his home in Spain wearing red bishop's robes and mitre and throwing oranges at people.[67] One of his assistants is Zwarte Piet ('Black Pete'), who is often featured in world press every year for the stubborn use of a black face as part of the traditional costume, while carrying a bag of sweets to throw at children. This is rooted in the story of how Saint Nicholas threw gold coins into the stockings of three young girls so they wouldn't have to work as prostitutes.

In Siberia, Christmas trees and other conifers can survive environmental temperatures of -60°C – and even liquid-nitrogen-induced laboratory temperatures of -196°C – by temporarily turning to glass. In their glassy crystalline state, the trees can't move or react, their metabolism drops to zero, and their cells aren't damaged by the extreme cold. The process is known as 'hardening'.[68]

You need a crossbow to climb one of the world's tallest trees. The Doerner fir, the tallest Douglas fir in the world at 99.7m tall, doesn't have branches until *c*.60m up, and so tree climbers use crossbows

---

67. Even this, I would say, does not make for the title of strangest bishop. This, I think, is enjoyed Bishop John Noonan, who is the Catholic Church's current Bishop of the Moon. In accordance with the 1917 Code of Canon Law, any newly discovered territory falls under the purview of the diocese from which the expedition set off. Therefore, in the eyes of the Church the Moon is technically part of the Diocese of Orlando, Florida.

68. You can do the same thing with tortoises, to optimise their hibernation. Taylor and Marshall Veterinary Practice of Shifnal, Shropshire, UK, offers the service of storing the live tortoises of clients in their refrigerators for 6-12 weeks over winter, making sure to occasionally open the door for airflow. 'We have got 37 coming this year,' vet Liz Hanson told the BBC in 2021, adding, 'I think I've probably got about another 10 at my house.'

or giant slingshots to set climbing ropes. The Doerner fir and its neighbouring Douglas firs in Oregon on the west coast of the USA are so large that they have their own ecosystems at their crown. Endangered spotted owls, flying squirrels, red tree voles and even clouded salamanders have been found existing up there for entire generations without ever touching the ground.

Rudolph the red-nosed reindeer is female, as are all the other reindeers that pull the sleigh of Father Christmas. We know this by the way they are always depicted as having antlers. Male reindeer use their antlers to fight each other during the autumnal breeding season, but by Christmas they have cast them off. Only females retain them through the winter period.

Paris once ate the zoo. The strangest Christmas dinner ever held took place in 1870 in Paris during the Franco-Prussian War, when the city found itself being starved into submission by surrounding enemy forces. Butchers had been selling cutlets of rat, cat and horse for weeks, but for Christmas Day, the ninety-ninth day of the siege, as an act of defiance chef Alexandre Etienne Choron (1837-1924) at the restaurant Voison decided to do something special. The Jardin des Plantes zoo had lost some of its animals to enemy bombardments and, as the city starved, the rest were sacrificed for the sustenance of the citizenry. Choron gathered what he could and arranged a unique menu (shown below). Dishes included head of a stuffed donkey, elephant consommé, roast camel, kangaroo stew, bear ribs, wolf haunch, cat garnished with rats, antelope terrine with truffles and watercress salad. 'Yesterday, I had a slice of Pollux for dinner,' wrote Henry 'Du Pré' Labouchère (1831-1912), an English writer and politician in Paris at the time. 'Pollux and his brother Castor are two elephants, which have been killed. It was tough, coarse, and oily, and I do not recommend English families to eat elephant as long as they can get beef or mutton.'[69]

The Voison menu during the ninety-ninth day of the Siege of Paris, 1870.

---

69. While eating the meat may not be recommended, other uses have been made of elephant remains – Edward VII owned a golf bag made from an elephant penis.

PREMIÈRE COMMUNION DE JEUNES FILLES CHLOROTIQUES
PAR UN TEMPS DE NEIGE

First Communion of Anaemic Young Girls in the Snow (1883) is
a painting by the French humourist and artist Alphonse Allais
(1854-1905), a participant in *Les Arts incohérents* movement,
producing witty absurdist satire. Decades before John Cage
composed 4'33", a musical piece in which the performers are
instructed not to play their instruments at all, Allais wrote the first
known example of a silent musical composition. Funeral March
for the Obsequies of a Great Deaf Man (1897) is comprised of
24 blank measures.

In 2021 Italian artist Salvatore Garau sold his sculpture *Io Sono*
('I Am') through the Italian auction house Art-Rite, a sale that
raised eyebrows because the sculpture was 'immaterial'; or in
layman's terms, he managed to sell a square metre of nothing.
'You don't see it but it exists, it is made of air and spirit,' he
explained. 'After all, don't we shape a God we've never seen?'
The unnamed buyer paid €15,000.

There is a curious phenomenon in marine law known as a 'Doughnut Hole'. Doughnut Holes occur when the zones of nautical sovereignty of two countries overlap intermittently at points, leaving occasional pockets of international water between the two nations. In the Gulf of Mexico, several of these Doughnut Holes, or 'Hoyas de Dona', were formed, and quickly became a point of contention between the USA and Mexico as the gulf's oil fields are especially bountiful, and crucial to both countries. In 1997, as the two countries readied a treaty, Mexican authorities noticed that maps since the sixteenth century had shown a tiny Mexican island named Bermeja right in the centre of these Doughnut Holes and realised that, by confirming its location, they could lay claim to the region's oil. Expeditions were sent to find the island continually until 2009, when a team of experts finally concluded that the island had never existed.

'Zero stroke' or 'cipher stroke' was a disorder reported by physicians in Germany during the era of hyperinflation in the Weimar Republic in 1923. Patients compulsively wrote endless rows of zeros, brought on by the daily requirements to calculate commercial transactions in the billions and trillions, making it virtually impossible to do business in Mark banknotes. Paper money lost so much value that notes were used as wallpaper.

William Shakespeare's *Much Ado About Nothing* is a title with a multifaceted pun. 'Noting', which was pronounced similarly to 'nothing', meant spying and overhearing, gossip and rumour, which is a theme of the play. In addition to this, in Elizabethan England 'no-thing' was slang for vagina, derived from women having 'no thing' between their legs.

'Nothing-books' are published works that appear to address a serious subject but are filled with empty pages as a joke. A gentleman named Sheridan Simove had a best-selling hit in 2011 with *What Every Man Thinks About Apart from Sex*, a book of 200 blank pages. The idea dates back at least as far as the nineteenth century, when the Scottish MP William Montagu Douglas Scott (1831-1919), Earl of Dalkeith, was ridiculed by a blank pamphlet titled *The Political Achievements of the Earl of Dalkeith* (1880). Around the same time Mark Lemon (1809-1870), founding editor of the magazine *Punch*, published *Advice to Those Intending to Marry*, with its contents of just one word: 'Don't'.

Nothing is an uninhabited town 190km northwest of Phoenix, Arizona. It was founded in 1977, and had a population of four at its height. It was abandoned in 2005. The town sign reads:

Town of Nothing Arizona
Founded 1977 Elevation 3269ft

The staunch citizens of Nothing are full of Hope,
Faith and Believe in the work ethic. Thru-the-years
these dedicated people had faith in Nothing, hoped
for Nothing, worked at Nothing, for Nothing.

In the evolution of life on Earth, from 1.7 billion years ago, nothing much happened for the next billion years. This period is referred to in academia as the 'Boring Billion', when Earth existed as a world of algae and microbes, with blue-green cyanobacteria feeding off the carbon dioxide in the atmosphere and gradually releasing oxygen. Then, 750 million years ago, glaciers spread, complex animals developed and nature picked up the pace.

Everything is almost entirely nothing. Only
c.0.00000000000000000000042 per cent of the universe contains
matter, which is made of atoms, and over 99.99 per cent of every
atom is composed of nothing but empty space.

The ancient Greeks did not have a number for zero – according to
Aristotle (384-322 BC), it was not possible to divide by nothing and
get a meaningful result – and neither did the Romans, who did not
incorporate nothing into their numeral system. This is why there
are not 1000 years between 500 BC and AD 500, but 999, because
the formulation of the Anno Domini system between the sixth and
ninth centuries drew on Roman numerals, which meant there was
no year 0. Our calendar goes from 1 BC to AD 1.

The worldwide change from the Julian calendar to the Gregorian
calendar, which is still used today, was a gradual one over centuries.
When Pope Gregory XIII (1502-1585) issued the papal bull in 1582
decreeing the adoption of the Gregorian calendar, only five countries
took it up: the Italian principalities, Poland-Lithuania, Portugal,
Spain and most of France. It also necessitated the discarding of days
to bring it back in synch with the time it takes Earth to complete
an orbit of the Sun. In North America, for example, September
1752 had only nineteen days – 2 September was followed by
14 September. Japan cut twelve days from 1872; while Russia,
Greece and Turkey switched calendars only in the early twentieth
century, which meant they had to jettison thirteen days.

William Strachey (1819-1904) was an English civil servant who lived in Calcutta for five years working for the Colonial Office. From his time there he was convinced that Indian clocks were the most accurate chronometers in the world, and so when he returned to England he simply refused to give up living by Calcutta time. The remaining sixty years of his life in England were lived six hours ahead of everyone else. A candlelit breakfast at *c.*3 a.m., lunch at breakfast time and so on.

At the Paris International Exposition of 1867 Strachey bought a new invention: a mechanised bed primed by an alarm clock that tipped the occupant out onto the floor to wake them up. Strachey set it up so that it would roll him directly into the bath. Apparently the first time this happened the shock of it made him so angry that he smashed the clock so that it couldn't happen again. He spent the rest of his life wearing galoshes, and when he died his nephew inherited his enormous collection of multicoloured underpants.

Between the seventeenth and nineteenth centuries 'sundial cannons' were a popular way of marking noon. The midday sun was focused by magnifying glasses to ignite gunpowder that fired a cannon. The Palais Royal in Paris used one daily; the last working example is in Åtvidaberg, Sweden.

A sundial cannon.

'Noon' used to mean 3 p.m. It comes from the Latin phrase *nona hora* ('ninth hour'), which was one of the seven fixed prayer times in medieval Christian tradition. By the fourteenth century the meaning of the word had shifted to midday.

'Back in a jiffy' is an expression for a vaguely short amount of time, but a jiffy is also a real scientific unit for the amount of time it takes for light to travel one fermi, or about a quadrillionth of 1m. Also, a moment is about 90 seconds – 'moment' is also an actual unit, used by medieval European astronomers to compute planetary movements.

Tomorrow will always be the longest day of your life. Billions of years ago a day on Earth lasted thirteen hours. Since then the Moon has been edging incrementally away from us at a rate of 38mm every year. This is because the friction from tidal drag ever so slightly reduces the energy with which the Earth rotates, while the Moon gains energy from this, moving it into slightly higher orbit. As Earth's rotation slows, its days get slightly longer.

The indigenous Aymara people of the Andes and Altiplano regions of South America have a concept of time that is a mirror image of our own: the past lies ahead, and the future lies behind. The Aymara word for 'past' is *nayra*, which literally means 'eye', 'sight' or 'front'. The word for future is *q'ipa*, which means 'behind' or 'the back'. The word *q'ipüru* ('tomorrow') combines *q'ipa* and *uru* (the word for 'day'), to create the meaning 'some day behind one's back'. Time, to the Aymara, is felt as motion, and speakers face the past, with their backs to the future.

SOME CURIOUS DEATHS
BEFORE WE'RE FINISHED

24 February 1525 Master of King Francis I's Horseguards, Galeazzo da Sanseverino (*c.*1458/1460-1525) is decapitated at the Battle of Pavia, but is so firmly attached to his saddle that his corpse continues to ride around the battlefield, terrifying the Spanish soldiers.

31 December 1610 Death of Ludolph van Ceulen (1540-1610), a German-Dutch mathematician from Hildesheim, who collapses from exhaustion having spent the majority of his life calculating the numerical value of π. He published his calculation of the number to an astounding thirty-five decimal places, a figure of such accuracy that it goes beyond any practical use. Following his death, π is referred to as 'the Ludolphine number' in Germany until the early twentieth century. His figure '3.14159265358979323846264338327950288 ...' can be found engraved on his tombstone.

6 November 1632 Gustavas Adolphus (1594-1632), King of Sweden, dies at the Battle of Lützen after refusing to put on his chest and back plates, declaring 'The Lord God is my armour' before leading a cavalry charge.

8 January 1687 The Italian-French composer and dancer Jean-Baptiste Lully (1632-1687) stabs himself in the foot with his conducting staff during a performance. The wound turns gangrenous, but the master of the French Baroque style refuses to have his foot amputated so that he can still dance. He dies from gangrene in Paris shortly afterwards.

15 March 1731 Death of Countess Cornelia Zangari Bandi (1664-1731) from suspected spontaneous human combustion. Her maid enters her bedroom to discover a pile of soot with just her legs below the knee, three fingers and the front of her skull.

6 June 1800 Death of Peter Labilliere (1725-1800), a British army major, who in accordance with his instructions is buried vertically upside down on Box Hill, Surrey, reportedly because he believed the world to be 'topsy-turvey' and this would lead to him being righted in the afterlife; and also to emulate St Peter, who was crucified upside down.

30 December 1811 Death of three-year-old Ninette von Fahrenheid, daughter of East Prussian noble Baron Friedrich Heinrich Johann von Fahrenheid (1780-1849). Obsessed with ancient Egyptian culture and their afterlife beliefs and rituals, the grieving baron orders the construction of a great pyramid in the Luschnitz forest near the Polish village of Rapa to be his family mausoleum. He has Ninette's body mummified and laid to rest inside. Over the next thirty-eight years, the remains of five more Von Fahrenheid family members are put through mummification and laid inside the Pyramid of Rapa, the last being the baron himself.

11 January 1854 Californian teen named William Snyder (c.1840-1854) suffers a pulmonary rupture while 'being swung by his heels by a circus clown', according to the San Francisco, El Dorado County and Tehama County cemetery records of 1850-1862.

6 June 1867 Death of Archduchess Mathilde Marie Adelgunde Alexandra of Austria (1849-1867) from accidental self-immolation at Hetzendorf Palace. Having dressed in a gauze dress to go to the theatre, she lights up a forbidden cigarette. Hearing her father approaching, she hides it behind her back, which ignites the dress and she goes up in flames in front of her entire family. Her funeral procession is held at night by torchlight.

17 June 1871 American lawyer Clement Laird Vallandigham (1820-1871) attempts to prove his client's innocence of murder by demonstrating how the deceased man accidentally shot himself by discharging a pistol while trying to pull it free. While pulling the gun from his own waistband, Vallandigham inadvertently shoots himself in the stomach. His client is found not guilty, and Vallandigham dies in hospital the next day.

25 October 1920 King Alexander of Greece (1893-1920), uncle of Prince Philip, Duke of Edinburgh, dies of sepsis after being bitten by a palace steward's pet monkey.

26 April 1926 After becoming the second person to survive riding inside a barrel over Niagara Falls, the English daredevil Bobby Leach (1858-1926) later dies after slipping on some orange peel in the street in New Zealand.

2 November 1944 Midgley Jr (1889-1944), American inventor of leaded petrol, chlorofluorocarbons (CFCs) and a hundred other patented products, is found dead in his home in Worthington, Ohio, apparently strangled by one of his own inventions devised to assist him in getting out of bed.

16 February 1974 A coroner's inquest concludes that the death of a 48-year-old health-food enthusiast named Basil Brown (*c.*1926-1974), whose skin was bright yellow at the time of expiration, was caused by 'carrot juice addiction'. The court hears evidence that the golden Mr Brown had taken 70 million units of vitamin A in the preceding ten days, in addition to the 4.5 litres of carrot juice he drank daily.

22 April 1988 American veteran parachuting instructor Ivan McGuire, 35, with a record of over 800 successful jumps to his name, leaps out of a plane with a student to film their skydive. Only then does Maguire realize that he has mistaken the heavy video equipment he's wearing for the parachute that he's left behind on the plane. He does not survive the 10,500-foot fall.

22 August 1995 The first wild otter seen in the UK for almost forty years is discovered by a naturalist in Nottinghamshire, who then accidentally runs it over with his car.

15 November 1997 A Vietnamese man creeps up on his wife and tickles her as she chops firewood. She jumps and hurls the axe, which almost completely decapitates him and he dies soon after in hospital. When police arrest 62-year-old Siek Phan she explains: 'I hate being tickled.'

15 November 1998 A Portuguese dance teacher named Alberto Fargo tangoes straight out of a fifth-floor window to his death. Lisbon police explain that Fargo was showing his class how to keep the head high by looking at the ceiling and did not see the open window.

☠

IN THE END ...

This is the earliest known painting of the end of the world, as seen on the night of 7-8 June 1525 by the German artist Albrecht Dürer (1471-1528) in a vivid dream. When he awoke he immediately put it to canvas. In *Dream Vision; a Nightmare* he notes:

> I had this vision in my sleep, and saw how many great waters fell from heaven. The first struck the ground about 4 miles away from me with such a terrible force, enormous noise and splashing that it drowned the entire countryside ... When I arose in the morning, I painted the above as I had seen it. May the Lord turn all things to the best.

While envisioning future disasters, Nostradamus (1503-1566) also wrote a recipe for his own Love Jam. In *Traité des fardemens et confitures* (1555), a book of recipes for makeup and jams, he reveals that to make his Love Jam one needs the blood of seven male sparrows, mandrake apples and the eyelets from the arms of an octopus preserved in honey. 'If a man were to have a little of it in his mouth,' he wrote, 'and while having it in his mouth kissed a woman, or a woman him, and expelled it with his saliva, putting some of it in the other's mouth, it would suddenly cause ... a burning of her heart to perform the love-act.'

Should the world end in the manner predicted by the Bible, then anyone near the small English market town of Bedford would do well to head to a modest, end-of-terrace house on Albany Road, where a house was kept empty for Jesus Christ in the event of his Second Coming. The Panacea Society was a religious group founded in 1919 by Mabel Barltrop (1866-1934) of 12 Albany Road, who declared herself Octavia, the daughter of God, and who believed Bedford to be the original site of the Garden of Eden. The group built a small following with staggering assets; by 2001, when the society was selling off property for tax reasons; they were worth £14 million.

The New Fire ceremony was performed by the Aztecs every fifty-two years to mark the end of a full cycle of the Aztec 'calendar round', when the fear was that the Sun might not return. Hearthstones were thrown out as part of a 'spring clean', and all existing fires were extinguished. The Aztecs then lit a fire on the chest of a sacrificial victim and cut out his heart to fuel it. They would also add to the fire by cutting their ears and pouring their blood onto its flames, and then rekindle their own fires from the flames of this human hearth.

In ancient Egyptian mythology Apophis, deity of evil, chaos and opponent of light, routinely attacks the barge of the sun god Ra as he sails through the night. Rather worryingly, Apophis is due to make a return to Earth. On Friday 13 (when else?) April 2029, an enormous asteroid sharing the name is expected to narrowly pass by within 31,000km of Earth's surface. A flyby of an object of this scale only occurs every thousand years or so.

Choosing how to bring things to an end is a delicate art. At parties, for example: writers told of how the Roman boy-Emperor Elagabalus (c.203-222) would invite guests to lavish dinners at his palace, where wine would flow freely. When his guests were drunk, Elagabalus found it hilarious to have lions and tigers locked in the room with them to maul them to death. The authors of the *Historia Augusta* also mention the ending of one dinner party in which the teenage psychopath had tonnes of violets and other flowers released from a vaulted ceiling, in such quantities that his guests suffocated beneath them.[70]

---

70. Which recalls the story of a party thrown in 1906 in Philadelphia by Mary Astor Paul (1889-1950), who had the idea to surprise her guests by releasing 10,000 butterflies from ceiling nets. Unfortunately, as she pulled the release cord, she wasn't aware that, in the time it had taken for the guests to arrive, the insects had all perished from the heat of the lamps.

Stanley Kubrick's black comedy *Dr Strangelove or: How I Learned to Stop Worrying and Love the Bomb* (1964) could have looked very different – the original filmed ending consisted of an eleven-minute custard-pie fight between the world leaders in the war room. The entire sequence was cut from the final print.

William Shakespeare's *The Tragedy of King Lear* (1605-1606) was rewritten in 1681 by Nahum Tate (1652-1715), who wanted a cheerier ending. Unlike Shakespeare's original, Cordelia is given a love story with Edgar and ends up on the throne in a sentimental, happily-ever-after conclusion. Tate's perkier version was the one performed on English stages until it was completely phased out by 1838, when Shakespeare's original script was officially reinstated.

The eighteenth-century antiquarian John Warburton (1682-1759) built a collection of around sixty handwritten manuscript copies of plays performed by Shakespeare's troupe The King's Men. Many of the scripts were unpublished and included otherwise unknown works by Shakespeare (1564-1616), Christopher Marlowe (1564-1593), Philip Massinger (1583-1639/1640) and William Rowley (*c.*1585-1626). Unfortunately, Warburton chose to store his collection in his kitchen. When he decided to dig them out a year later, he discovered that only three remained – the rest had been used to line baking tins by his cook Betsy. 'After I had been many years collecting these MSS. Playes,' he wrote, 'through my own carelessness and the ignorance of my servant in whose hands I had lodged them, they was unluckely burnd or put under pye bottoms.'

The oldest surviving copy of Seneca's satire *Apocolocyntosis (divi) Claudii* ('The Pumpkinification of (the divine) Claudius') was written out by a scribe at the Fulda Monastery, Germany, in *c*.800. In it, Seneca tells us, six lines from the end, that Claudius's final words were: 'Oh dear, I appear to have shat myself.'

And finally, remember to respect a good ending, especially if books are the only thing keeping you sane. In 2018 a Russian scientist ended a four-year-long stint with a colleague at the Bellingshausen station on King George Island in Antarctica by stabbing the man with a kitchen knife. As his colleague was being treated, Sergey Savitsky, the first person to be charged with attempted murder in Antarctica, was asked why he attacked him. He said that he was fed up with the man spitefully telling him the endings of all the books he was planning to read.

SOME INTERESTING QUOTES TO LEAVE YOU WITH

'Make your wet dreams come true!'

US presidential campaign slogan of Al Smith (1873-1944), in reference to his promise to repeal Prohibition.

•

'Umbrella of the love god.'

Literal translation of smart-chatra, the Sanskrit word for clitoris.

•

'Heavier than air flying machines are impossible.'

Lord Kelvin, president of the Royal Society, 1895.

'Tails, tails!'

Taunt of the people of Paris hurled at the English soldiers vacating the city in 1436, after a sixteen-year occupation. From the twelfth century to the sixteenth century, it was a popular belief that Englishmen were born with short, deer-like tails that they kept hidden beneath their clothing.

•

'Went for a walk.'

Note left behind after a vending machine disappeared on Capitol Hill, Seattle, USA, on 29 June 2018.

•

'A mid-air collision can ruin your whole day.'

Approach: The Naval Aviation Safety Review, 1958.

•

'May your sky be filled with clouds.'

Iranian blessing

•

'This was certainly a strange and disturbing event.'

Ottoman explorer Evliya Çelebi (1611-1682), after learning that the gift of some noticeably 'hairy' honey he had gratefully devoured had not been taken from a goatskin container, as he had assumed. Instead, his Circassian host explained that he had collected it from his own father's coffin situated high up in the trees, where honeybees had colonised the dead man's groin.

•

'The wide one.'

The literal translation of 'Plato', the nickname given to the ancient Greek philosopher by his wrestling coach that he then adopted as a pen-name. His real name was Aristocles.

'At one point, it declared, out of nowhere, that it loved me.
It then tried to convince me that I was unhappy in my marriage,
and that I should leave my wife and be with it instead.'

New York Times journalist Kevin Roose on his conversation with the
Bing AI chatbot 'Sydney' in February 2023.

•

'There are certain things which are not jokes, Gogarty,
and one of them is my hanging.'

A condemned Lord Dunsany to Oliver St John Gogarty,
after the latter attempted to cheer up his friend by reminding
him of a peer's privilege of being hanged with a silken rope,
and joking on its probable elasticity.

•

'The wind has blown and the anus of the chicken
has been exposed.'

Nigerian proverb for how hidden things eventually
come to light.

•

'Those children of mine.'

The weary sigh of Middlesbrough Stipendiary Magistrate
Mr. H.S. Mundahl, after taking a pencil from his pocket in court to
record his first decision on 1 April 1930, and finding that the pencil
was a joke one made of rubber.

•

'Caved in, my arse. It had a bloody boot-print on it.'

Response of competitive pumpkin-grower Pete Glaze to rival Barry
Truss, who denied putting his foot through Mr Glaze's prize entry
and told reporters that it must have caved in naturally, in the
English village of Beckbury, Shropshire, in 2011.

'He sings, plays on the violin wonderfully, composes, is mad.'

Horace Walpole (1717-1797) describes his encounter with the mysterious society figure the Count of St Germain, who claimed to have discovered the secret to eternal life, and to have attended the wedding at Cana where Jesus turned water to wine.

•

'SUGGEST YOU UPSTICK BOOKS ASSWARDS.'

Ernest Hemingway's telegrammed response to the request from his editor for a detailed summary of his expenses.

•

'I'm the luckiest guy in the world. The Lord is on my side.'

The words of Marion Barry, mayor of Washington D.C., to a female companion, seconds before police and FBI agents crash through his hotel room door after watching him purchasing and smoking crack cocaine via a hidden camera on 18 January 1999.

•

'Could he have been smarter about the way he tried to cover things up? Yes, he could have.'

Statement by Deputy Prosecuting Attorney Stacey Slaughter at the trial of James Newsome or Fort Smith, Arkansas, USA, who robbed a convenience store while wearing an orange hard hat with his name written on the front in 1999.

•

'I've fallen in love or imagine I have; went to a party and lost my head. Bought a horse which I don't need at all.'

Leo Tolstoy's diary entry on 25 January 1851.

•

'I live!'

The last words of Roman emperor Caligula (AD 12-41).

PICTURE CREDITS

P7 Wikipedia; P18 Wellcome Collection; P23 (bottom) British Rail; P27 Library of Congress; P30 NASA; P32 Courtesy NASA/JPL-Caltech; P33 NASA/JPL/ Dan Goods; P36 Wikipedia.co.uk, One half 3544; P40 Wikipedia.co.uk, Alexrk2, NordNordWest; P55 Wellcome Library; PP60-61 US National Library of Medicine; P63 Musée des Beaux-Arts de Quimper; P68 Getty Images.co.uk; P70 Vladislav Rogozov Yuri Vereschagin; P71 Ahmed Shafik; P75 Museum of Science and Industry; P77 J. Paul Getty Museum; P79 Jorg Bittner Unna; P82 Wellcome Library; P83 Museo Ideale Leonardo da Vinci; P84 Gov.uk; P86 ウィキ太郎 (Wiki Taro); P92 San Diego Air and Space Museum Archive; P101 Library of Congress; P108 Wiki Commons; P112 Nagaraju Raveender; P114 Library of Congress; P121 North Dakota State University Libraries; P125 US Patent and Trademark Office; P130 PA Images / Alamy Stock Photo; P138 Ernst Mayr Library, Harvard University Museum of Comparative Zoology; P142 Kmhkmh, Wiki Commons; P145 US National Archives and Records Administration; P149 (top) Zoological Society of London; P153 Brendan Lynch; P154 Rijksmuseum; P156 Frank Janssen; P165 Himalayan Art Resource; P166 Seville University Library; P171 Ake Axelsson, wikipedia.co.uk; P179 Humboldt University Library; P182 Mobilus In Mobili; P183 (bottom) Photo courtesy of and © Belvedere, Wien. Creative Commons Licence CC BY-SA 4.0; P184 British Library; P187 Cobatfor wikipedia.co.uk; P191 British Library; P196 Ambras Castle; P197 (top) Det Kongelige Bibliotek in Copenhagen, Denmark; P203 Imperial War Museum; P204 (top and bottom) US National Archives and Records Administration; P205 New York Post; P207 Smithsonian; P209 Centre d'Enseignement et de Recherches de Médecine Aéronautique; P211 Jorbasa Fotografie/Flickr/Creative Commons; P212 Glenbow Museum Archives; P214 Meccano Magazine; P215 US National Archives and Records Administration; P224 Osama Shukir Muhammed Amin FRCP (Glasg); P225 Sailko, Wikipedia.co.uk; P226 British Library; P228 Sam van Aken, Ronald Feldman Fine Art; P229 National Gallery of Art; P232 British Library; P234 National Palace Museum, Taipei; P243 Waseda University Library; P244 Juntaku, Wiki Commons; P249 Jkfcfriedchix, Wiki Commons; P259 US National Archives and Records Administration; P262 Otourly; P266 National Numismatic Collection, National Museum of American History at the Smithsonian Institution; P267 Library of Congress; P273 Getty Research Institute; P278 NOAA photo library; P279 Zeno.org; P282 (top) The Bishop Museum; P283 (top) British Library; P283 (bottom) University of Göttingen; P286 Library of Congress; P293 NTB / Alamy Stock Photo; P295 Fitzwilliam Museum; P300 Gallica, Wiki Commons; P304 Rama, Wikipedia.co.uk; P310 Kunsthistorisches Museum.

All other images are the author's own or public domain.

Every effort has been made to find and credit the copyright holders of images in this book. We will be pleased to rectify any errors or omissions in future editions.

ACKNOWLEDGEMENTS

I would like to express my deep appreciation to all who provided such indispensable help in the creation of this book: to Charlie Campbell at Greyhound Literary; to Alison Macdonald at Simon & Schuster UK; to Laura Nickoll and Keith Williams for yet another beautiful design, and to Joanna Chisholm. With many thanks to my family for all their support; to Annie Jump Cannon without whom I would have finished this book so much faster; and to Alex and Alexi Anstey, Matt, Gemma, Charlie and Wren Troughton, Kate Awad; and to my friends at QI, John Lloyd, Dan Schreiber, Andy Hunter Murray, Anne Miller, Sandi Toksvig; and Jason Hazeley. The most interesting people in the world.

First published in Great Britain by Simon & Schuster UK Ltd, 2024

Editorial Director: Alison MacDonald
Project Editor: Laura Nickoll
Design: Keith Williams, sprout.uk.com

3 5 7 9 10 8 6 4

Simon & Schuster UK Ltd
1st Floor
222 Gray's Inn Road
London WC1X 8HB

www.simonandschuster.co.uk

Simon & Schuster Australia,
Sydney

www.simonandschuster.com.au

Simon & Schuster India,
New Delhi

www.simonandschuster.co.in

A CIP catalogue record for this book is available from the British Library

Hardback ISBN: 978-1-3985-3237-3
Ebook ISBN: 978-1-3985-3238-0

Printed and bound in the UK using 100% renewable electricity
at CPI Group (UK) Ltd

MIX
Paper | Supporting
responsible forestry
FSC® C171272
www.fsc.org